CITY OF LIGHT

ALSO BY RUPERT CHRISTIANSEN:

Prima Donna: A History

Paris Babylon

*Romantic Affinities: Portraits from an Age
1780–1830*

*The Victorian Visitors: Culture Shock in
Nineteenth-Century Britain*

CITY OF LIGHT

THE MAKING
OF MODERN PARIS

RUPERT CHRISTIANSEN

BASIC BOOKS
New York

Basic Books
Hachette Book Group
1290 Avenue of the Americas, New York, NY 10104
www.basicbooks.com

Printed in the United States of America

First Edition: October 2018

Published by Basic Books, an imprint of Perseus Books, LLC, a subsidiary of Hachette Book Group, Inc. The Basic Books name and logo is a trademark of the Hachette Book Group.

The Hachette Speakers Bureau provides a wide range of authors for speaking events. To find out more, go to www.hachettespeakersbureau.com or call (866) 376-6591.

The publisher is not responsible for websites (or their content) that are not owned by the publisher.

Print book interior design by Trish Wilkinson.

The Library of Congress has cataloged the hardcover edition as follows:
Names: Christiansen, Rupert, author.
Title: City of light : the making of modern Paris / Rupert Christiansen.
Description: First edition. | New York : Basic Books, 2018. | Includes
      bibliographical references and index.
Identifiers: LCCN 2018012387 (print) | LCCN 2018033758 (ebook) |
      ISBN 9781541673434 (ebook) | ISBN 9781541673397 (hardcover)
Subjects: LCSH: Paris (France)—History—1848–1870. | Urban
      renewal—France—Paris—History—19th century. | Public works—
      France—Paris—History—19th century. | Haussmann, Georges
      Eugáene, baron, 1809–1891—Influence.
Classification: LCC DC733 (ebook) | LCC DC733 .C483 2018 (print) |
      DDC 944/.36107—dc23
LC record available at https://lccn.loc.gov/2018012387

ISBNs: 978-1-5416-7339-7 (hardcover), 978-1-5416-7343-4 (ebook)

LSC-C

10 9 8 7 6 5 4 3 2 1

*En mémoire de Claudine, Nicole,
Danielle, et les autres chères filles au pair de
mon enfance, qui m'ont inspiré une ardeur
romantique pour la ville lumière*

CONTENTS

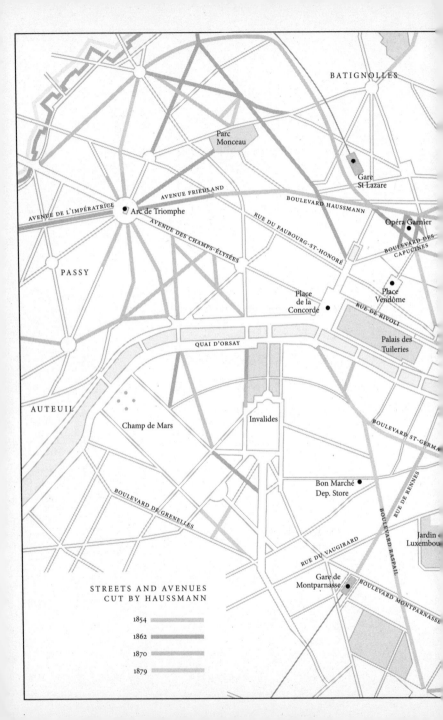

BATIGNOLLES

Parc
Monceau

Gare
St Lazare

AVENUE FRIEDLAND

BOULEVARD HAUSSMANN

AVENUE DE L'IMPÉRATRICE

Arc de Triomphe

Opéra Garnier

RUE DU FAUBOURG-ST-HONORÉ

BOULEVARD DES
CAPUCINES

AVENUE DES CHAMPS-ÉLYSÉES

PASSY

Place
Vendôme

Place
de la
Concorde

RUE DE RIVOLI

QUAI D'ORSAY

Palais des
Tuileries

AUTEUIL

Champ de Mars

Invalides

BOULEVARD ST-GERMA

RUE DE RENNES

Bon Marché •
Dep. Store

BOULEVARD DE GRENELLES

BOULEVARD RASPAIL

Jardin
Luxembou

RUE DU VAUGIRARD

STREETS AND AVENUES
CUT BY HAUSSMANN

Gare de
Montparnasse

BOULEVARD MONTPARNASSE

1854
1862
1870
1879

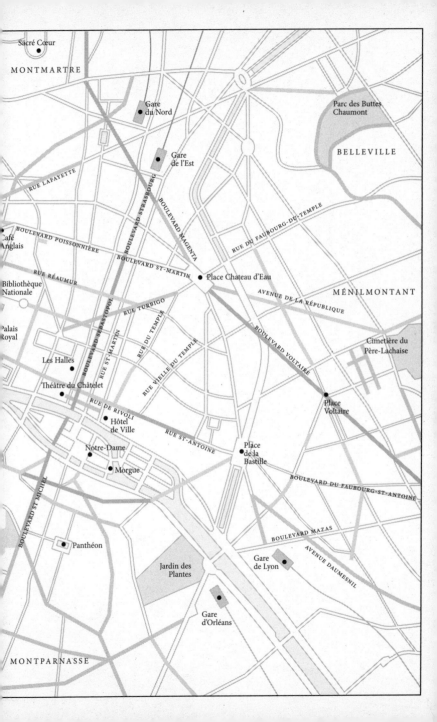

A view of the foyer of Garnier's Opéra as it is today.
(Joe Vogan / Alamy Stock Photo)

PROLOGUE

JANUARY 5, 1875, WAS A winter's evening during which Paris radiated all the glamour that had earned it a reputation as *la ville lumière,* the city of light. Tonight would be special: a brighter glow in its celebrated illuminations was caused by the ceremonial opening of a magnificent new opera house, designed by the architect Charles Garnier in a style of unabashed grandeur that continues to astound and delight today. The occasion of its inauguration drew hordes of rubberneckers to the streets as a pageant of officers of state, crowned heads, venerable nobles, and uniformed dignitaries paraded through the doors. A particular sensation was caused by the arrival of the lord mayor of London, emerging from a gilded fairy-tale coach robed in all the antique splendor of his office.

An artist's impression of the foyer of Charles Garnier's Opéra on its opening night, January 5, 1875. (EVERETT COLLECTION / BRIDGEMAN IMAGES)

The building had been under construction for nearly fifteen years at vast cost, with no expense spared on either materials or decoration. But for the moment, nobody cared about the budget sheet (several million francs over the original estimate, as is so often the case): a week before, Garnier had formally handed over the 1,942 keys to the management,

Garnier's Opéra, as seen from the Avenue de l'Opéra, circa 1880. (PRIVATE COLLECTION / BRIDGEMAN IMAGES)

and now the singers and dancers prepared to christen it in a lengthy program of operatic scenes and balletic *divertissements*. To a city addicted to excitement, scandal, and headlines, the novelty was all: as *The Times of London* reported, the opening of the Opéra was "the sole, the only topic which engages public interest and attention."

The show proved something of an anticlimax, dragging on interminably without aesthetic distinction. Exacerbated by opening-night panic and production problems, the scenery did not fit the space properly, and the stage management proved amateurish. The prima donna Christine Nilsson had withdrawn at the eleventh hour, as prima donnas tend to do, because of "an indisposition." As the exasperated critic Léon Escudier wrote in his review, "A corner grocer's shop could have organized a more attractive artistic celebration." There were problems of protocol as well: so lengthy was the list of honored guests that Garnier, the genius who had fanatically devoted himself for over a decade to the creation of this wonder of the world, was assigned a seat in a box to the side of the auditorium on the second tier, an appalling snub that he brushed aside by choosing to remain in his office and continue working instead.

This was the public's first glimpse of the foyers where Garnier's imagination had run free: gilded and mirrored salons, shimmering candelabra and marbled colonnades, ceilings covered with mosaics and frescoes, classical statuary, and flaming gas torchères, all enhancing a superb central stairwell that turned the ascending and descending audience into a spiraling spectacle far more impressive than anything that the clunking grand operas and silly, twittering ballets could display on stage. Patriotic hearts were exhorted to rejoice, and even the satirical weekly *Le Sifflet* responded to the call: "Be proud of being French when looking at our Opéra! Foreigners who come to visit this marvel will see that despite all our misfortunes, Paris is and always will be without rival."

Yet ultimately the significance of this opera house was not a matter of music, art, or even architecture. It was an ideologically charged symbol of France's recent history and bruised national pride: an ambiguous monument to a triumph and a disaster that had started as one thing and ended as another.

The project had originated as a key element of a vast, unprecedented strategy to redevelop the capital's center that was conceived by Louis Napoléon, authoritarian ruler of France from 1852 to 1870, and executed by his fearsomely effective left-hand man and de facto mayor of Paris, Baron Haussmann. An opera house would be a focal point for a network of new streets, new private housing, new public buildings and monuments, new parks, new sewers, and even new city boundaries that ranks among the greatest experiments in urban planning ever undertaken.

But in 1870 the French had foolishly gone to war against Prussia and suffered a crushing and unexpected defeat. Louis Napoléon's regime, known as the Second Empire, had collapsed, and Paris had in consequence endured a long siege, followed by a revolt that resulted in the brief establishment of the socialistic Commune, suppressed by the new republican government through a swift massacre of perhaps 20,000 French citizens.

By this time, Haussmann had lost his job, victim of his own high-handedness. Although much of the master plan that he gave to the capital would continue to be realized for a time, the fate of Garnier's Opéra hung in the balance. A humbled France was bound to pay a huge indemnity to Prussia after the war, and public funds were scarce. Given those circumstances, many believed that it was profoundly wrong to dedicate scarce resources to the completion of a pleasure palace that symbolized the ostentatious hedonism and frivolity of the Second Empire's culture.

But with three-quarters of the work already achieved by 1870 and much of the remainder already commissioned or paid for, it was too late to cancel or even substantially reconsider Garnier's scheme, and as if to end the debate, Paris's grand opera house on the Rue Le Peletier burned to the ground in 1873. So after Garnier accepted a face-saving budget cut and made several minor but politic alterations, including removal of the imperial insignia from the facade, the theater was ready for business. It swiftly proved a triumph, hailed internationally as a wonder, and even today it remains a fully functional home for opera and ballet as well as being a popular tourist attraction.

Those who turned away in moral disgust could console themselves with the construction by public subscription of a white monument in Montmartre, at the highest point of the city, on ground literally stained by the recent violent turmoil. The foundation stone for the Basilica of Sacré-Coeur (as it would eventually be consecrated in 1919) was laid only a few months after the opening of the Opéra,

The Basilica of Sacré-Coeur under construction.
(Keystone-France / Gamma-Keystone / Getty Images)

and its purpose could hardly have been more different: built on austere Romano-Byzantine principles, the basilica represented an overt penance for the war with Prussia and the crimes associated with the Commune, as well as an implicit rebuke of the sins and errors of the Second Empire. A shrine of traditional Catholic piety and doctrine, it would be devoted to orthodox worship, sober reflection, and spiritual regeneration.

The basilica and the opera house, embodiments of the sacred and the profane, were two buildings that looked strangely backward, reflecting from opposite ends of the moral spectrum a quarter century of the most tumultuous physical and political change that the city had ever known. How had this schism erupted, and where should this chapter in Paris's story begin?

1

LOUIS NAPOLÉON AND THE SECOND EMPIRE

SINCE THE STORMING OF THE Bastille in 1789, France had suffered continual political instability: different constitutions, dynasties, and ideologies were constantly jostling for power as models of empire, monarchy, and republic were adopted and rejected, sometimes with violence and always over-shadowed by the wayward course of wars with the rest of Europe. The Revolution of 1789–1794 had gathered a terrifying momentum as it intensified from moderate demands for constitutional reform under the Bourbon Louis XVI to the high-minded republicanism of the Girondins to the radical dictatorship and murderous populism of the Jacobin Terror. The more conciliatory but insecure regime of the Directory followed, its weakness allowing the rise of the successful General Napoléon Bonaparte to the rank of consul and then self-appointed emperor in 1804. All this within fifteen years.

What ensued was no less tumultuous as Napoléon won and lost territory that extended as far as Moscow. At Napoléon's downfall, the monarchy was restored as Louis XVI's brothers Louis XVIII (1814–1824) and Charles X (1824–1830) established a repressively conservative and Catholic culture that led to a further outbreak of revolution in Paris in 1830.

From that unrest came a more liberal constitutional monarchy: Louis-Philippe of the House of Orléans, a man bourgeois in personal style and mollifying in political temperament, took a newly conceived and circumscribed throne validated by a narrow electorate of the propertied class. But fierce opposition from various extreme factions was constant, and he survived seven assassination attempts before abdicating and fleeing to England in 1848. Poor harvests, high unemployment, a mismanaged economic slump, and political unrest among a radicalized youth had sparked another bloody outbreak in Paris that led to another republic being declared, based on high hopes and universal male suffrage.

Who could lead France now? Enter the stocky, unassuming, and unprepossessing figure of Louis Napoléon, born in 1808 as the son of Napoléon's brother Louis and of Hortense de Beauharnais, the daughter of Napoléon's wife, Josephine, by her first marriage.[1]

After Napoléon's downfall, all members of his dynasty were banished from France, so Louis Napoléon's childhood was itinerant: Switzerland, Germany, Italy, Britain. After Napoléon's son died in 1831, Louis became the great hope of the Bonaparte dynasty, a position that consolidated a burning idea that it was his destiny and his right to rule France. He expounded his mission in various pamphlets and polemics, claiming to be the man who could rise above party and faction to unite the nation on the basis of a vote made by universal male suffrage.

During Louis-Philippe's feeble and compromised reign, Louis Napoléon won a ready hearing: with corruption rife throughout the incompetent administration, there was growing support for a return to the strong central government of the Bonapartes. In 1836 Louis Napoléon planned a coup: it failed humiliatingly, and he had a lucky escape. After trips to Brazil and the United States, he settled for a couple of years in London. Living off the fortune of his late mother, he strolled daily through the city's parks and admired the sweep and vision of John Nash's great scheme of shops and housing that stretched down Regent Street to Carlton House Terrace.

In 1840 he landed at Boulogne to attempt a second coup. It proved another hopeless flop, verging on the farcical. Louis Napoléon was arrested and sentenced to life imprisonment in the château of Ham in Picardy. Here he spent six years in moderately comfortable circumstances, entertaining guests—including the mother of his two illegitimate children—and writing a variety of articles on social and political issues as well as a popular book focused on the problem of poverty and its elimination. In 1846 he managed without much difficulty to disguise himself and escape, returning to London for two further years, during which he socialized with the likes of Disraeli and Dickens. Always one for the ladies, he now took up with the worldly and wealthy courtesan Harriet Howard, who remained his mistress for several years and funded his political ambitions.[2]

When revolution erupted in February 1848, Louis Napoléon literally swapped places with Louis-Philippe: on the same day that the latter left

Paris under the assumed identity of "Mr. Smith" for exile near London, Louis Napoléon set out to cross the Channel, confident that his moment had come. In fact, he was a few months premature: in the wake of riot and bloodshed, with only the most fragile of provisional governments sustaining the declaration of a republic based on the 1789 cry of *Liberté, Egalité, Fraternité,* he held back from staking his claim—wisely as it turned out, because another wave of street violence erupted in June, plunging the city back into a nightmare of barricades, slaughter, and mass arrests.

Leaving others to sort out the mess and lose their reputations in the ensuing recrimination, Louis Napoléon kept his distance from the fray until a round of elections in September, when he was elected by a large majority to the new National Assembly; sick of reforming liberals, radical socialists, and reactionary monarchists, the peasantry and working class voted overwhelmingly for a Bonapartiste candidate promising national unity and a return to the good old days when Napoléon was a strong-arm ruler and France was Europe's dominant nation.

The new government prepared a constitution that included an elected president. With a convincing show of humility and florid expressions of being motivated by nothing except a desire to serve France to the best of his ability, Louis Napoléon offered to stand as a candidate in the presidential elections of December 1848. His populist manifesto promised— as such manifestos invariably do—stability, justice, and prosperity for all, with particular reference to interventions designed to improve the lot of the poor without stinging the rich through a socialist redistribution of property. Buttressed by an efficient campaign that reached throughout the country, this hollow rhetoric convinced the voters: he won by a staggering margin, gaining almost three-quarters of the vote, defeating candidates from across the political spectrum, including the idealistic poet Alphonse de Lamartine, the pacifist leader of the provisional government who opposed the death penalty and campaigned for the right to work.

But the title and powers of president of the Second Republic of France would not be enough for him, not least as the new constitution forbade him to stand for a second term. With the stealth and cunning that always characterized his political behavior, he hatched a quiet plan to reestablish his regime on a more permanent footing. To placate liberal and leftist factions, he initially swore to uphold democratic institutions and appointed several republicans to his cabinet, only to sack them one by one shortly afterward. His propaganda insisted on identifying nameless plots and underground conspiracies ready to foment anarchy, the threat they posed being sufficient to necessitate stiffer police powers and repressive measures. Meanwhile, he appeared in public in the uniform of a general (to which he had no legal right) and planted cheerleaders in crowds who noisily hailed him not as president but as emperor—the Napoléonic honorific. The army's loyalty was assured through a hefty pay raise.

Having thus tested the water—and controlled its temperature—he enacted a swift coup d'état in December 1851. Another demagogic revolution threatened France, he proclaimed, and there was no alternative to a state of emergency if order was to be maintained. As he had guessed, the inevitable opposition could be managed and its noisier dissidents dispatched to prisons or penal colonies. He was now "prince president" of the Second Republic, endorsed by a massive majority after another national referendum: well over 7 million in favor, some 600,000 against, and 1.7 million abstentions. Enraged by what he saw as an act of outright tyranny perpetrated by someone he had initially supported, the great poet and novelist Victor Hugo left France and would not return for twenty years: from his base in the Channel Islands, he would publish a scathingly satirical pamphlet titled *Napoléon le petit* that made him the new regime's most prominent ideological enemy, albeit one with no firsthand experience of it.[3]

But Louis Napoléon knew he had an unbeatable mandate. He set to work amending the constitution to give himself new powers that would see him elected to a renewable ten-year term, with the independence of parliamentary institutions vastly reduced and the scope of the opposition minimized. One of his more-trivial measures was a prohibition on students at universities growing full beards, excessive hirsuteness being regarded as a sign of red republican tendencies.

Further stage-managed elections ensured that the right people were in command of the right positions, and in October 1852 the prince president made a tour of the provinces, giving a keynote speech in Bordeaux that set out his vision of a France made newly prosperous through a vast development of its infrastructure: "We have immense uncultivated territories to clear, roads to open up, ports to construct, rivers to make navigable, canals to complete, a railway network to finish . . . everywhere we have ruins to restore, false gods to overthrow, truths to make triumphant."[4]

The roars of approval that greeted such rhetoric emboldened him further. The Senate was sharply nudged to propose that the Second Republic should be replaced by the Second Empire and that the prince president be crowned Napoléon III, emperor of the French. This was put to the electorate, and another referendum delivered the necessary landslide. The field was clear.

∽᳁ᴄ∾

WHO WAS LOUIS NAPOLÉON? NOBODY altogether knew. Genuinely mild mannered to the point of blandness (Karl Marx dismissed him contemptuously as "a grotesque mediocrity"),[5] he became one of those second-grade dictators who avoid heavy-handed gestures and prefer being liked and admired to being feared and loathed. He was flexible; he was ready to listen and to hold back. He was never excessively vindictive or bloodthirsty, and he preferred taming his enemies to coercing them— exile to Algeria was his preferred punishment for serious political offenders, and even they were eventually offered pardons. He countenanced neither torture nor extortion, and although his means were often deeply unscrupulous, he was perhaps justified in terms of his end: the domestic stability of the Second Empire allowed a genuine extension of France's material prosperity.

Nor can he be accused of megalomania: he accepted that at some point in the future he would be wise to relax his grip and allow genuine democracy to prevail. In an address made shortly after his coronation in 1853, he said: "To those who regret that a greater share has not been allotted to liberty I reply: liberty has never helped to found an enduring edifice: it crowns it when time has consolidated its existence."[6] True enough, surely—especially in a country that could scarcely serve as an advertisement for the benefits of *liberté*.

Three principal strategies secured his position. The first involved providing a simulacrum of democratic institutions—a senate, an independent judiciary, councils, elections, consultation, and representation—without permitting them any teeth or claws. They were merely talking shops; the making and enacting of all significant decisions were centralized in Louis Napoléon's personal office. Yes, you could expect a fair trial and adult males were enfranchised with a vote, but boundaries were gerrymandered, there was no secret ballot, and in rural areas peasants (often illiterate) were strongly advised by the presiding mayoral officers to select the "official candidate," who was the only one permitted to use white paper. Yes, there was parliamentary debate, but members of legislative bodies could be dismissed at the emperor's whim. Yes, there were amnesties for troublemakers, but only on condition of signing an oath of loyalty to the Empire.

The second strand was a cunning system of censorship that could almost pass for reasonable tolerance and relied more on self-censorship than a strictly enforced code. The rules were vague: you could say and write what you liked as long as it did not incite disorder or flout decency—the definitions of which could be freely determined by the police. Cafés, cabarets, and other dives in which heretical talk might ignite unrest were kept under surveillance, and clubs with any sort of political agenda were banned. The chief news agency, Havas, was in effect an arm of the Ministry of the Interior, issuing an official version of the truth and editing out anything that did not fit the message. Stamp duty on all publications was increased, and caution money had to be lodged as a deposit against fines for anticipated future infringements of the code. Such measures discouraged opposition, to say the least.[7]

However, it was Louis Napoléon's third focus that had the most striking impact. He spent huge amounts of public money. Following his uncle's adage that "a new government must dazzle and astonish,"[8] he decided that the Second Empire would not oppress its citizens so much as awe them, not only through what it constructed in bricks and mortar but also in terms of sheer theatrical spectacle, parade, pageantry, and exhibition—one big long party or "succession of miracles," as his Minister of the Interior Victor, duc de Persigny, proposed: "The public must be overawed by the almost uninterrupted occurrence of prodigies due to the presence of one man."[9]

The first necessity was to ensure loyally cheering, flag-waving crowds wherever the emperor appeared in public. This could be arranged easily enough in the provinces and rural areas where Louis Napoléon's support was most solidly based; in more skeptical Paris, some adroit news management via favored journalists was required, for the actual reception might be thin or even hostile. But from cannon-saluted visits from foreign royalties and triumphant military marches to openings of railway lines, canals, bridges, fountains, and envelopes, no opportunity to make a speech, blow a trumpet, or pull open a curtain was missed.

During the reign of Louis-Philippe, the "Citizen King" of the 1830s and 1840s, the court had dressed down in an attempt to make itself popular by avoiding palatial extravagance. But now, under a Grand Maître des Cérémonies, the duc de Cambacérès, gilded splendor was reinstated with an uninhibitedly lavish vulgarity not seen since the days of Marie Antoinette. Liveries of Louis XIV, complete with knee breeches and white stockings, were specified for gentlemen, while ladies were encouraged to imprison themselves in vast crinolines that displayed the marvels wrought by French seamstresses, embroiderers, and lace makers. The emperor's gestures were munificent: titles and honors were doled out at pompous investitures conducted at his official palatial residence of the Tuileries, and sumptuous if tedious weekend house parties were held at the imperial château in rural Compiègne. These were much mocked by the intelligentsia, but of course everybody longed to go, and from Mad King Ludwig of Bavaria to Gustave Flaubert and Louis Pasteur, nobody ever turned down an invitation.[10]

An artist's impression of a Second Empire ball at the Tuileries Palace (now demolished). (Musée de la Ville de Paris / Musée Carnavalet, Paris, France / Bridgeman Images)

No matter of protocol required more sensitive attention than that of the succession to the throne. The survival of the dynasty depended on a healthy son and heir: Eugénie duly produced such a boy and then appears to have turned away from the marital bed, perhaps disgusted by Louis Napoléon's infidelities or perhaps out of a general distaste for the whole business of sex. Born in 1856, Napoléon Eugène Louis Jean Joseph—blush-makingly always known in the family as Loulou—was adored and cosseted by his middle-aged father, whose health was not good and who must have sensed that he would not live long enough to fulfill his grand plan for France's future. Every stop would therefore be pulled out to keep Loulou sturdy and educate him into welcoming his destiny. Making it clear that the child was indisputably consecrated meant that his baptism was a matter of consummate political importance.

The christening was held in a Nôtre-Dame freshly restored by the celebrated Gothic revival architect Eugène Viollet-le-Duc and illuminated with a shimmer of 10,000 candles that flickered magically over the new stained-glass windows. Loulou's godfather was the pope; his godmother was Queen Victoria. Five thousand guests were invited, or at least that was the figure that was given out to the press.[11] At nine months, Loulou was admitted as an honorary member of a regiment of guards and given his first military uniform; at the age of six, he was made a corporal and began accompanying his father to military reviews. Distinguished academics and stern generals were engaged to tutor him in the schoolroom. The boy would grow up dutiful and earnest, a keen rider and fencer, but charmless and unintelligent. All eyes were on him: how could he fulfill so many expectations, hopes, and dreams?

Louis Napoléon's *fête impériale* would not come cheap. Even at low interest rates, borrowing from banks could not meet the bill, and the need to raise further money by parliamentary consent would prove the one great check on his power. For the first years of the regime, the idea that growing national debt could be offset by higher tax receipts generated by increased economic activity and easy credit was plausible, and in boom years nobody worried much. Later, the balance sheets of an economy spiraling out of control would begin to cause widespread alarm and disaffection. But politically it continued to make good sense: apart from providing the mass employment that had been so lacking

Louis Napoléon, his wife Eugénie, and their son, Louis, the prince impérial, misleadingly presenting themselves as an ordinary middle-class family. (ROGER VIOLLET COLLECTION / GETTY IMAGES)

under Louis-Philippe, it helped France to appear confident in itself, not only to its own people but also to a world gazing at its glamour with wonder and envy.

2

THE PROBLEM OF PARIS

AT THE HEART OF EVERYTHING Louis Napoléon did and thought about was the question of Paris. Because of his long exile, it was not a city he knew well or even particularly liked (London was much more to his personal taste), but he knew that the success of his regime would be measured in the way that his policies played out there. Like all dictators, he feared his capital's restive energy and combustible proletariat, those forces that had ignited the revolutionary explosions of 1789–1794, 1830, and 1848 and that could not be controlled by ordinary policing. He had the sense to understand that jobs were the key to order and loyalty: "I would rather face a hostile army of 200,000 than the threat of insurrection based on unemployment."

Paris was the key. Aside from its political volatility, the place was in a dismal state of physical decay, its oases of splendor such as the Louvre and the Arc de Triomphe surrounded by a fetid wilderness of filth, stench, and crime, pitted with noxious warrens of tortuous backstreets cramped with decrepit tenement housing and swarms of wretched humanity. The population had almost doubled since 1800. Major outbreaks of cholera, spread by contaminated water, had claimed tens of thousands of lives in 1832 and 1849. Traffic ground to a halt in daily gridlocks as the infrastructure creaked and cracked. The sum of it was a crisis that could only get worse.

There had been much tinkering with the problem over the years, and many grand reports and bold proposals had been submitted. In the 1780s Louis XVI had mapped the city and decreed a code specifying approved dimensions for new buildings; in 1793 a commission was established to address matters of congestion and street width. A decade later, Napoléon constructed the arcaded Rue de Rivoli, running from the Place de la Concorde alongside the Tuileries and the Louvre. Under Louis-Philippe, in the wake of the 1832 cholera epidemic, further practical initiatives were undertaken. The comte du Rambuteau, prefect of the Seine and therefore in effect Paris's mayor, had commissioned a new Hôtel de Ville, completed work on the Arc de Triomphe, and built new sewers and water conduits as well as demolishing buildings in a particularly rough area of the Right Bank to create a long, straight, broad avenue, running east-west from Les Halles to the Marais and lined with gaslights and planted with trees: today it is still known as the Rue Rambuteau.

However, Jacques Lanquetin, a veteran of Waterloo and a wine merchant who led the city council from 1848 to 1852, urged something even more radical and visionary. Piecemeal or isolated schemes were no good, he insisted, and at a width of 12 meters (40 feet), the Rue Rambuteau was too narrow for the pressure of its regular traffic; plans for the city's future streets had to be wider, integrated, and systemic in order to be effective. The advent of the railways was about to transform demographics and necessitate entirely new lines of communication and circulation to and from the terminals. Tolls should be abolished and the food market of Les Halles moved out of the center, but at this point Lanquetin was shouted down: where would the money come from? Paris prided itself on balancing the books and living off its revenues, chiefly taxes on property and levies (known as *octroi*) on goods entering the city. What was being proposed would entail massive expropriation and the payment of equally massive compensation, all to be negotiated through complex legal process; without imprudently large loans, the sums simply did not add up.[1]

Louis Napoléon was having none of it: a drastic remedy was required, and there was no time to lose. In brief, he used his power grab to dismiss Paris's timid naysaying governors and ensure that legislation simplifying compulsory purchase was waved through (basically, the financial terms were generous, but there could be no appeal). Capital could be raised by borrowing from the banks—themselves liberalized—on the economic basis that the development would provide employment and raise rents and land values, thus generating growth and returns. Louis Napoléon believed that Paris had a lot to learn from Nash's grand master plan for London, but the British had to be trumped—on his watch, he would aspire to make the French capital rank again as the most beautiful and exciting city in the world.

Where was the deputy who could be entrusted with this daunting brief, the fine details of which he could not attend to himself? Not, certainly, Prefect Rambuteau's successor, the stolid and legalistic Jean-Jacques Berger, who would be let go. It was in Bordeaux that the regime found its man: here in 1852 Louis Napoléon had made a highly successful official visit, immaculate down to the last fluttering pennant and trumpet fanfare, all organized by the prefect, a career civil servant named Georges-Eugène Haussmann, whose record was impeccable.

⁓◦⁓

BORN IN 1809, HAUSSMANN SPRANG from a solid and steady middle-class Protestant Alsatian background; his forefathers included several senior public servants of a Bonapartist persuasion. Imposingly tall, handsome, and muscular, he had nevertheless suffered in his Parisian childhood from choking asthma, an affliction that might go some way toward explaining his subsequent obsession with clearing blockages and opening up airflow. He enjoyed a progressive education in a fashionable lycée, where he numbered the poet and dramatist Alfred de Musset among his friends. His own bent was musical—he was an accomplished cellist and lifelong opera fan—but he chose to study law at the Sorbonne before entering civic administration. Working his way through several provincial postings, he proved himself a supremely disciplined and organized pragmatist, as charming as he needed to be in pursuit of his goals, but signally lacking in tact or respect for petty protocol.[2]

In his memoirs, Haussmann related that he received the telegram announcing his appointment at a civic dinner. "I took care to hide my great surprise," he said, quietly folding the paper into his pocket and informing the gawping company that it was "nothing serious."[3] But he must have been expecting something: Louis Napoléon's people had long earmarked him as potentially useful, and he had been subject to a long, secret grilling by Interior Minister Persigny, whose main concern was to test the extent of Haussmann's loyalty to the imperial idea. Persigny remembered the meeting vividly:

I had before me one of the most extraordinary types of our time. Large, powerful, vigorous, energetic, and at the same time sharp, shrewd, resourceful, this bold man was not afraid to show himself for what he was. With visible self-satisfaction, he put before me the highlights of his career, sparing me nothing: he would have

Baron Haussmann, a giant of a man. (WIKIMEDIA COMMONS)

talked for six hours without stopping as long as it was on his favourite subject, himself. Far be it from me to complain of this tendency. It revealed all the sides of his strange personality. Nothing could be so curious as the way he told me about all his titanic struggles . . . above all with the municipal council of Bordeaux. While he was informing me in the greatest detail of the incidents in his campaign against formidable adversaries in the municipality, the traps he had set them, the precautions he had taken to make them fall into them, then the stunning blows he had given them once down, his face lit up with triumphant pride.

While this absorbing personality spread itself before me with a sort of cynical brutality, I could not hide my keen satisfaction. To fight against the ideas, the prejudices, of a whole school of economics, against the shrewd, sceptical men of affairs come for the most part from the lobbies of the Bourse or the corridors of the courts, and not very scrupulous about the means they used, here was the man for me. Where the most intelligent, clever, upright and noble men would inevitably fail, this vigorous athlete, broad-shouldered, bull-necked, full of audacity and cunning, capable of pitting expedient against expedient, setting trap for trap, would certainly succeed. I rejoiced in advance at the idea of throwing this tall tigerish animal among the pack of foxes and wolves combining to thwart the generous aspirations of the empire.[4]

Haussmann was never officially named the mayor of Paris because Louis Napoléon was wary of such a title; it would have been too dangerous to give any single person the power that it implied. Instead, like his predecessors, he was called prefect of the Seine, ranking equal alongside the prefect of police of the Seine, with whom lay matters of security and the prerogative to arrest, impound, and enforce. But that suited Haussmann, who had other ways of dealing with obstacles: he did not want or need to get involved with the police or even with politics, with its inevitable negotiations, compromises, and retreats. His sole interest was organization and efficiency, his genius being limited to the logical and methodical procedures whereby one could move from A to B until one reached Z. Problems were there to be solved; opposition was there to be ignored or circumvented. His talents were purely managerial: he had no partisanship, no imagination. Haussmann was the emperor's servant, empowered to get a tough job done, and that was the sum of it.

On June 29, 1853, the day that Haussmann was officially installed into office, he attended a formal luncheon, followed by his first private interview with Louis Napoléon. Here Haussmann claimed that he showed his mettle at once, rejecting the idea of instituting an official commission of planning and making it plain that he intended to let the municipal council lie fallow. The only seal of approval he recognized was the emperor's. All he wanted was some basic instructions. At this point Louis Napoléon produced a map (sadly, it has not survived) he had roughly sketched out in blue, red, yellow, and green crayons indicative of priorities, outlining a network of new boulevards that would cut through the city's clogged arteries and allow it to breathe more freely. Through the next seventeen years this chart would remain the template.

Henceforth, Louis Napoléon and Haussmann would meet constantly. No record of their conversations survives, and posterity must depend on Haussmann's unabashedly self-serving memoirs for evidence of how they operated. However, it was said that only the prefect of police had the same level of immediate regular and confidential access to the imperial inner sanctum and that the intimacy of their daily meetings whenever Louis Napoléon was in residence in Paris became a source of resentment to other ministers and supplicants. Both in their different ways possessed of cool and inscrutable personalities, their relationship remained purely professional, not least because Louis Napoléon's ghastly wife thoroughly disliked Haussmann, thinking him vulgar or at least insufficiently groveling. Haussmann did not care: to his credit, he was never a courtier, always a civil servant, and if the two men did not embrace each other, they did not quarrel either.

Haussmann's working habits in the Hôtel de Ville were rigorously disciplined, starting at 6 A.M. The great majority of his day was spent sitting calmly in his sumptuously appointed office, patiently attending to detail and holding brief decisive meetings: not one to waste words, he relied on his phenomenal memory and the efficiency with which he processed the paperwork. Preferring not to involve himself unnecessarily with the humanity of the streets, he paid only the minimum of visits to construction sites and never left his carriage to wander or chat: what the man on the Courbevoie omnibus felt about things meant nothing to Haussmann. In the words of historian David P. Jordan, "He had little tactile contact with the city . . . it was not a living organism with habits: Paris, had, for Haussmann, needs but no desires, limbs and arteries, a digestive system, but no heart."[5]

With his staff he was relentlessly strict and impeccably fair, entirely unloved but greatly respected. What made him most fearsome was the knowledge that he was incorruptible and unmoved by the prospect of personal monetary gain. His income was relatively modest, his expenses transparent: in the evenings, he and his mousy, ignored wife entertained in high style, as befitted his status, but every *sou* was accounted for. Bribes left him cold, even when relatives were offering them—favors worth hundreds of thousands of francs were rejected with a shrug. His shortcoming, a fatal one, was his arrogance: he was not an overt bully, and he listened carefully while assessing a situation, but he was right about everything, contemptuous of those who crossed him and dismissive of their arguments. People like him tend not to have friends: friends serve only to make the tough decisions so much harder.

Having established his management style and examined the budget, he hired and fired ruthlessly. Being a shrewd judge of people, he sacked a lot of idle placemen and subsequently remained loyal to those he appointed—several of his closest deputies would remain in their posts even after his own departure. At his right hand was an unprepossessingly disheveled but unflappable architect and surveyor named Eugène Deschamps, who embodied much of Haussmann's own single-mindedness: he was given the Herculean task of assembling the first-ever comprehensive map of Paris, fully triangulated and on a scale of 1:5,000. This great work, to which Deschamps dedicated himself fanatically, would take three years to complete. Much-smaller versions were produced for public sale, but the original measured 15 square meters (160 square feet). Mounted on a screen behind Haussmann's desk, it dominated his office. "Many an hour have I spent in fruitful meditation before this altar," he later recalled.[6] Using this as his guide, Haussmann then commanded the leveling of Paris—the elimination of all obstructions, bumps, and dips that would have interfered with his precious straight lines and long vistas. This procedure often required feats of delicate and complex engineering; one early and notable example was the suspension on timber scaffolding of the entire Tour St Jacques, a venerable monument standing on a hillock where the Rue de Rivoli met the Hôtel de Ville: after the ground beneath was flattened, it was lowered back down onto a new base—at the total cost of more than 500,000 francs.[7]

With such preliminary tasks completed, the greater work could now begin on a scale previously unimagined.

MUCH OF THE FIRST WAVE of development had already been planned and approved by the city authorities when Haussmann took office, so the credit he can take for it is based on what today we would call "project management." The construction of the elegantly arcaded Rue de Rivoli, started by Napoléon Bonaparte and continued under Charles X and Louis-Philippe, was being extended east; the Louvre was being connected to the Tuileries palace; the covered market at Les Halles was being rebuilt; and Louis Napoléon had his own pet project: the landscaping of the Bois de Boulogne in the English style of Lancelot "Capability" Brown.

However, Haussmann's immediate priority was to authorize the ruthless elimination of the chaos of crumbling tenements and stables in the Place du Carrousel (now the flat open square of the Louvre Pyramid). As a man who hated mess, he took enormous satisfaction in "clearing all that as my first job in Paris . . . since my youth the dilapidated state of the Place du Carrousel . . . seemed to shame France, an admission of impotence on the part of her government, and it stuck in my throat."[8]

Looking back, he might have deemed this the least problematic or controversial part of his mission. Much more testing would be the insertion of the first spoke in a vast wheel of wide boulevards designed above all to ease the flow of traffic to and from the railway stations that were fast becoming nineteenth-century Europe's hubs of trade and human passage. In a project that became known as *la grande croisée* (the great crossroads), Napoléon Bonaparte's extension of the Rue de Rivoli would be continued down the Rue Saint Antoine alongside the Marais toward the Place de la Bastille, traversing the reconceived Place du Châtelet at right angles to an entirely new boulevard, running north to south from the Gare du Nord and Gare de l'Est across the Île de la Cité and the Seine down through Montparnasse to the Porte d'Orléans—broadly speaking, the stretch now covered by the Boulevards de Strasbourg, Sébastopol, and Saint-Michel.

From the start, not everyone could see the need for this—why couldn't the extant and parallel Rue Saint-Denis simply be widened? But cutting corners and making small economies or compromises with minor objections were not in Haussmann's temperament, and he forged ahead. The first section of this grand thoroughfare would be inaugurated in 1858 with a terrific parade of tarantara typical of the Second Empire. At its intersection with the Place du Châtelet hung gold lamé curtains, suspended between 60-meter (200-foot) minarets and decorated with stars, diamonds, and imperial insignia, that were theatrically drawn up to the sound of trumpets as Louis Napoléon trotted down the route on horseback.[9]

Haussmann's passion for road building remained the core of his mission—not until Hitler's Autobahn program in 1930s Germany would anyone show comparably ambitious determination to improve the passage of traffic. Others, such as Rambuteau, had recognized the problem of Paris's sclerotic arteries but had balked at the challenge of doing more to unblock them: what was stunningly new about Haussmann's and Louis Napoléon's approach was its steamrolling progress through the thickets of physical obstacles and political opposition, as well as its holistic vision of a city with interlinking roads, railway stations, and property development in a massive strategy of social engineering.

Enshrined indelibly in legend is the idea that Louis Napoléon's secret agenda in extending the boulevards related to security. Like all such myths, it contains a grain of truth. Garrisons and barracks were located at key points along the boulevards, allowing cavalry to advance unimpeded and infantry to march in wide formation in the event of insurrection. Old Paris did indeed contain many uncharted places in which the disaffected or criminal could hide and plot, while broad streets, mapped, numbered, and brightly lit as public spaces, could not be swiftly barricaded with the ease that had allowed the revolutionaries of 1830 and 1848 to bring the city to a halt. But perhaps this was so obvious to everyone that it scarcely needed articulating, and it certainly was not a primary motivation of either Louis Napoléon or Haussmann; it would be more accurate to say that an ideology of efficiency was the impulse, making Paris a smoothly functioning machine that could be controlled and surveyed, generating the maximum of profit for a contented affluent citizenry controlled by a ruling élite.

Haussmann had an almost pathological hatred of blockage—one can detect in him symptoms of an obsessive-compulsive disorder—but his determination to clear human and vehicular circulation was also part of a broader economic strategy that envisaged the boulevards being lined with new retail and residential developments that would yield high levels of rent for entrepreneurs as well as increase employment and tax revenues for the city and state. The complex financial scaffold supporting this construction is a subject to which we shall return.

Despite the initial carping, *la grande croisée,* executed with stupendous efficiency and completed by 1859, was widely welcomed. Everyone's legs appreciated the long, clean, straight, smooth thoroughfares, with their generously broad tree-lined pavements; everyone's eyes enjoyed the artfully calibrated perspectives, interrupted at key points by open squares or circuses and monumental columns or domes; everyone's lungs benefited from the gutting, draining, and aerating of some of Paris's most noxious and dilapidated backstreets, home to cholera and crime. But the second phase of Haussmann's plan would prove more ambitious, expensive, and controversial.[10]

Through the 1860s, he developed a further 26 kilometers (16 miles) of boulevard. On the Right Bank this included the approaches to the Gare du Nord and Gare Saint-Lazare; the replacement of the slum known as *La petite Pologne* (Little Poland) with the Boulevard Malesherbes; and the creation of what is now called the Place de la République, fashioned out of a popular chaotic street full of low-grade theaters, dives, and vices known as the Boulevard du Crime (splendidly reimagined in Marcel Carné's 1945 film *Les Enfants du Paradis*), with three new avenues leading off it. Perhaps most magnificent was the frame provided for Napoléon Bonaparte's Arc de Triomphe, the focal point of the Place de l'Étoile, now flanked by twelve ascending satellite streets, crowned by a diadem of fine buildings of uniform scale and design fronted by identical patches of lawn and iron fences—"this lovely arrangement" Haussmann called it, stirred and satisfied by its neat symmetry and grandeur.

On the Left Bank, the Boulevard Saint-Germain was extended and the area around the Panthéon radically altered. But it was the Île de la Cité, sitting in the middle of the Seine, that underwent the most comprehensive reinvention. This was Haussmann's idea of hell—"a place choked by a mass of shacks," he wrote, "inhabited by bad characters and crisscrossed by damp, twisted and filthy streets"—and he attacked it vigorously. New bridges, the Pont Saint-Michel and Pont au Change, were constructed; the Hôtel-Dieu hospital and orphanage were rebuilt; there was massive clearance of the shambles that enshrouded Nôtre-Dame; and thousands of defenseless working people were expelled to make room for two imposingly expansive government buildings, the Tribunal de Commerce and the Prefecture de Police. At least Haussmann stopped short of demolishing the thirteenth-century Sainte-Chapelle, a Gothic masterpiece that constituted the last remains of the palace of the Capetian dynasty, and the gruesomely picturesque turreted prison of the Conciergerie, where Marie Antoinette, Charlotte Corday, and Robespierre were incarcerated before their executions. Yet what had been a place of messy human communities was eerily left as little more than a lifeless theme park showcasing authoritarian institutions. It has been suggested that Haussmann's vendetta was motivated by an element of personal neurosis: as a sickly asthmatic child repelled by dirt and terrified of foul air, he had traumatically been obliged to cross the Île from his home to school every morning.[11]

⌒ᗡᑪ⌒

IN 1860, FOLLOWING A DECISION only perfunctorily debated by consultative bodies and all too typical of his autocracy, Louis Napoléon demolished the inner Fermiers-Generaux wall[12] round the center and brought the suburbs of Paris directly under the administration and surveillance of the city. Eleven villages and townships outside the old wall were affected by this decree,[13] bringing the number of arrondissements from twelve to twenty, at which it remains today. Overnight this appropriation doubled the acreage of the city and increased its population by a third. In accordance

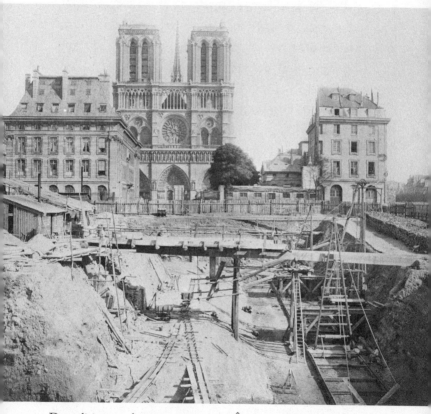

Demolitions and excavations on the Île de la Cité, creating a square that allowed a full view of the facade of Nôtre-Dame for the first time. (ROGER VIOLLET / GETTY IMAGES)

with the nineteenth-century belief in the virtues of free trade, the tolls and taxes that farmers had to pay to bring their produce through the gates of the Fermiers-Generaux into the center were thereby abolished, and Haussmann assumed responsibility for areas of heavy toxic industry, small agricultural backwaters, and virtually lawless stretches of scrub, neither rural nor urban, largely inhabited by impoverished, undocumented vagrants holed up in miserable shacks and sustained by petty crime and cheap alcohol.

Obliged to trudge daily miles to and from work in the center, much of this population eked out a wretched living on Haussmann's building sites. Some had been forcibly evacuated from the slums on the Île de la Cité; others came penniless from the countryside in search of employment. Few of the latter expressed any particular wish to be Parisian, and there was a certain resistance to the official attention and regulation that their new civic status entailed. The happiness of souls or the condition of morals was not something that concerned the unremittingly practical Haussmann, but furnishing this no-man's-land with basic social amenities such as cobbled roads, sewage disposal, street lighting, and water supply became his Herculean task. In the short term, the expense of the operation was a major drain on the city's financial resources; in the longer term, it would prove as transformational as anything else he achieved, shaping and civilizing areas now as organic to Paris as Auteuil, Batignolles, and Bercy.[14]

The problem to which neither he nor Louis Napoléon paid sufficient attention was housing the inhabitants of these outlying regions, and this would prove to be their biggest mistake at the levels of both basic humanity and political calculation (a mistake that many Western states are continuing to make in our own era). The majority of migrant families lived in the sort of hovels or shacks we would nowadays associate with the poorest parts of India: shelters cobbled together from wooden planks, sheets of corrugated iron, and anything else that could be foraged from dustheaps. Single men, if they were lucky, would be accommodated and fed in rough dormitories or vermin-ridden attics owned by the builders for whom they worked and to whom they would have to pay substantial rent.

At the time there was virtually no concept anywhere in Europe of direct state control over the provision of what we would now call social housing. This was a matter for individual enterprise,

Haussmann believed: let the market provide what the market wants, which in this case, as so often, resulted in a glut of high-end, high-rent housing along the new boulevards, umbilically linked in economic terms to abutting shops and businesses and accessible only to those who could raise a mortgage. One fault line at the heart of this has been forcefully summed up by urban scholar Anthony Sutcliffe:

> Haussmann had hoped that if the right conditions were created for building, free enterprise could provide sufficient accommodation for the very poor, and allow rents to stabilize. But by driving new streets through the centre, he did the opposite. Although he pointed out that the new buildings contained more dwellings than those that the City was demolishing, he conveniently ignored the fact that much of the land was not available for building after improvement, because it was incorporated in streets or open spaces. He also forgot that the older buildings were often let and sub-let room by room, whereas the new houses in the centre were divided into relatively spacious apartments and were, in any case, rarely occupied by the working classes.[15]

Louis Napoléon knew that there was a problem here, and he worried that a working class doomed to sordid living conditions could become politically disruptive. He favored a slightly more interventionist line, taking a benevolent if ineffectual interest in several schemes for *cités ouvrières* (workers' estates), inspired by the paternalistic socialism of Claude Saint-Simon, an early-nineteenth-century philanthropic thinker whose meritocratic ideas greatly appealed to him. But sufficient capital for these well-intentioned projects could never be raised, leaving *ateliers de charité*, run on workhouse lines by the church and restrictively governed by curfews and regulations, as the last resort of the destitute and the desperate.

⁓ဆၰ⁓

THE GREAT BULK OF HOUSING built during the Second Empire was squarely destined for the accommodation of the middle class. What financed it was a banking boom, at the head of which were two Sephardic Jews of Portuguese origin, the brothers Emile and Isaac Péreire. Bitterly controversial figures, they have been called many things—astute venture capitalists, brilliant visionary speculators,

The only extant photograph of the bidonvilles, the desolate slums encircling Paris, suggestive of the appalling living conditions that would give rise to the revolutionary violence of 1871. (ROGER VIOLLET / TOPFOTO)

ruthless profiteers—according to the ideological position of the observer. Beyond question they were the aggressive new presence in the Bourse, promoting through their chief creation, the Crédit mobilier, a concept of banking that was more open, daring, and wolfish than that of the more-refined, longer-established, and prudent Rothschilds. They took risks on innovation and enterprise, gambling heavily on all the growth areas of the mid-nineteenth century—railways, cabs and omnibuses, hotels, mining, insurance, gas, transatlantic shipping, and newspapers, as well as a loan to the government for the Crimean campaign of 1853–1856. Much of the time their daring paid off, buoyed by some highly creative accounting, gold rush money from America and Australia, and a generally optimistic economic climate.

Extending large-scale credit and allowing artisans and *petits bourgeois* to invest small amounts of their savings, the Péreires pumped money through Second Empire France and became the lifeblood of Haussmann's project. The government was only too happy to relax some restrictive regulations in Crédit mobilier's favor—taxation alone could never pay for its scale of ambition—and various wings and subsidiaries of the Péreires' empire took on direct responsibility for vast retail and housing developments. They were particularly prescient—some said, suspiciously so—in buying up undervalued land and building hotels around what would become the site of the new Opéra. For fifteen years they walked a tightrope until the economic slowdown in 1867 revealed the extent of their leverage and brought about a sharp crash. By that time, Haussmann had moved on, and, as we shall see, a lack of transparency in his hunt for capital would prove his downfall.[16]

Meanwhile, there were fortunes to be made in a system with plenty of room for the venal and unscrupulous standing in the path of progress to benefit from graft, corruption, and scams. Speculators second-guessed the routes of new roads and at bargain prices bought up land or freeholds that would double in value once their redevelopment was announced. Leaks of information from Haussmann's office in the Hôtel de Ville could not be plugged, even though the hands of Haussmann and his top echelon appear to have remained perfectly clean. Compulsory purchase orders also provided ordinary Parisians with a game that was easy to play, with a good chance of rich winnings. The rules were simple: you only had to be one step ahead. At the moment that an eviction notice was served on your property, you called in a crooked broker skilled in the dark art of making your premises look to the surveyors much better than the property did five minutes before it was condemned, either by importing some borrowed smart furniture to prettify a salon or cooking the accounts to suggest a booming trade. The broker would then skim off a percentage of the compensation, assessed by public juries all too ready to take bribes themselves in return for a favorable decision. Such practices contributed to an embarrassing overage of hundreds of millions of francs past the original budgets. In other respects they quelled opposition and made the job easier: Haussmann's schemes could be regarded as operating in many Parisians' narrow self-interest and short-term gain.[17]

⌒◦⌒

IF THE NAME OF HAUSSMANN means anything to the wider public today, it evokes the uniform rows of five- or six-story apartment blocks that run along the boulevards and avenues of central Paris. Much imitated all over Europe, they have become one of the archetypes of high-density urban domesticity, as resilient and flexible as the terrace villas that line London's Victorian suburbs. The middle classes like living in them; over two centuries they have weathered hardily and still do the job.

Many people must think that Haussmann designed the architectural template himself, but that is not the case. In fact, no single person can take the credit. One of the virtues of these buildings is that they are not highly or individually designed so much as evolved out of what was already there— the simple model being that of a shop or atelier on the ground floor, with flats of various proportions

The Rue de Rivoli, a project started under Napoléon Bonaparte and completed under Louis Napoléon—its clean, straight uniformity, smoothly running traffic, and pleasantly airy trees and parks all being aspects of Haussmann's ideal city. (L.P. Phot for Alinari / Alinari via Getty Images)

ascending over several levels to attics for servants and storerooms. In the Paris of the early nineteenth century, their frontage was typically narrow, perhaps 6 or 7 meters (20–23 feet) across, but the accommodation they offered could extend up to 40 meters (130 feet) deep; a long-standing city-wide regulation limited overall heights relative to street widths. Haussmann liberalized these dimensions in his boulevards, enabling a more general improvement in the circulation of air, traffic, and population.[18] A cramped and miscellaneous city was becoming a spacious and coherent one.

The broad lines of the "Haussmann style" were established in the 1840s, and only the professional eye can distinguish blocks erected during the last years of Louis-Philippe's reign from those of the early Second Empire (the Rue Rambuteau, for example, was built in the late 1830s). Haussmann had good if unadventurous taste, took an intelligent interest in new industrial technologies, and insisted on rigorous construction practices: he would not cut corners to save a few short-term francs, and everything commissioned during this era was built to last. Refining the aesthetic code for the new regime appears to have been the responsibility of an architect named Gabriel Davioud, working out of

Haussmann's office and also responsible for the design of much of the street furniture that graced the boulevards and parks, including the bandstands and ironwork.

Frustratingly, we do not know enough about the extent to which specifics were made compulsory because so much of the relevant documentation was destroyed by the fire that gutted the Hôtel de Ville in 1871. Nevertheless, what is clear from the surviving evidence is that the widespread notion that Haussmann's blocks are all the same is a delusion; whatever guidelines were set in the interests of an overall compositional unity, some room for difference and ornament remained. As architectural historian François Loyer put it, "Second Empire architecture has been criticized for the poverty of its mass effects and boring uniformity created by buildings of identical size, which is to overlook the fact that the monotony of the general forms was compensated for by an extraordinary variety of visual detail," most readily visible today in the decoration of window frames, lintels, corbels, and ironwork.[19]

The geometric principle underlying the new boulevards was a certain breadth in proportion to the regularized height of the buildings; in most cases, parallel lines of fast-growing plane trees were planted to provide enriching contrast with the grayness of the stone facades, cobbled roads, pavements, and curbs. Dressed and polished limestone from the quarries of the Oise region north of Paris, now conveniently transported as freight on the railways, became the standard building material (and regulations enforcing its decennial cleaning and maintenance have always been rigidly enforced on pain of a large fine). Roofs, slanting or curved, beneath which lodged the servant class in garrets or *chambres de bonne,* were traditionally made of zinc or slate; guttering was dark brown; and there could be no deviation from the sizes of windows that ran at fixed intervals across each floor of each block. But as a stroll along the Boulevard Saint-Michel can still demonstrate, richly nuanced differentiation in the shape of porticos, the ornament of their lintels and pediments, the modeling of pillars and caryatids, the framing of windows, and the patterns of balcony ironwork could happily be accommodated.

What is regrettable is that during the late 1860s, as the lion of capital ran rampant and roared ever louder, property developers became increasingly adept at bending and stretching the rules, building faster and cheaper with less attention to these decorative individualities. The result was a more stolid and unimaginative interpretation of the classical principles, marked by cruder carving and larger expanses of bare wall—this is particularly the case in outlying districts such as Ménilmontant, where overall coherence was less of an issue.

Behind the facades, what is most noticeable about the "typical" Haussmann apartment building (although it has been argued that there is no such thing) is a separation of class, status, and function much more rigidly hierarchical than had previously been usual. The shop on the ground floor no longer connected with the entrance hall to the residential levels; the common parts of stairwells and landings became progressively less grandiose and expansive as they ascended to the smaller flats on the upper floors; servants and trade came and went as surreptitiously as possible through a narrow back stairwell. Inside the apartments, the old idea of an enfilade of rooms, each of which might be used for sitting, eating, sleeping, and washing (or a combination of these), was replaced by a more defined pattern, partly dictated by the expansion of indoor plumbing and the water supply. Privacy, hygiene, and comfort were priorities: the pillars of the bourgeois lifestyle.[20]

3

MARVELS OF
THE NEW BABYLON

INTERIOR MINISTER PERSIGNY'S CALL FOR the
Second Empire to enforce itself by producing "a
succession of miracles" was a major request, and
most of what emerged—five town halls for the arrondissements, six barracks, two synagogues, four
new bridges across the Seine, 650 kilometers (400
miles) of new pavement, extensive planting of trees,
and the reconstruction of the Hôtel-Dieu, Paris's
central hospital—would be better characterized as
solidly utilitarian. More impressive were the trans-
formations made to the railway terminals, previously resembling warehouses or sheds, now rebuilt
like the Gare du Nord in a grandiose classical
style—cathedral-like in their naves, palatial in their

Victor Baltard's elegant sheds for Les Halles, the food market in the center of Paris. (HULTON ARCHIVE / GETTY IMAGES)

frontages, and designed to make innovative use of steel and glass.

An urgent priority was the rebuilding of Paris's food market: the antiquated sheds of Les Halles were awkwardly situated amid twisting streets that hindered deliveries and offered all too many opportunities for shifty vendors and suppliers to evade the stations for testing standard weights and measures. Shortly before Haussmann came to power, work had in fact begun on a new building by the distinguished architect Victor Baltard, designed in a classically colonnaded style that suggested a Roman temple rather than a place of commerce.

But Louis Napoléon did not like what he saw when he visited the site and decreed a halt until a more modern conception could be found, preferably one incorporating the arched iron girders and plate-glass panels that had been adopted for railway terminals and Joseph Paxton's Crystal Palace for the 1851 Great Exhibition in London. The emperor handed Haussmann a little pencil sketch of what he had in mind—"vast umbrellas, that's all," he said—and asked him to come back with some other architects' ideas along those lines.

Haussmann was left to carry the bad tidings back to Baltard, who considered himself a votary of Michelangelo and who bridled at the idea that he should be using iron rather than marble. Haussmann shrugged and told him to like it or lump it; the best thing he could do in the circumstances would be to return to his drawing board. Baltard duly produced three further designs attempting to minimize the iron girders and maximize the stone pillars. Each time, Haussmann sent him back and sternly told him to provide what he wanted. There was more complaining of the "I am an artist" variety, but Haussmann was actually on Baltard's side, and the hectoring worked.

Haussmann returned to the emperor and slyly presented him with a sheaf of faulty proposals from architects who had perhaps not been fully briefed about the emperor's wishes. A lot of head-shaking, hemming, and hawing ensued as they reached the bottom of the pile without finding an appropriate plan, but then Haussmann diffidently mentioned that he had one more proposal to offer. Let me see it, said the emperor. Without mentioning the architect's name, Haussmann produced Baltard's revision. "Ah, *enfin*," said the emperor. "Exactly what I wanted!"[1]

This is how the relationship between Haussmann and Louis Napoléon generally operated, to both parties' satisfaction and perhaps to the benefit of all—like so much that went on in the Second Empire, it was not quite corruption, but it was not altogether above board either. But things got done, and done properly and swiftly: the happy outcome of this little subterfuge was a fine set of efficient and commodious buildings that lasted for more than a hundred years.[2]

∽ঙৎ∽

THE CROWNING ARCHITECTURAL MIRACLE OF THE
Second Empire was a new opera house, built at
the intersection of a new avenue leading north from
the Louvre and the east-west Boulevard des Capucines. A project financed at enormous expense by
the state rather than the city of Paris, it represents
the zenith of the Second Empire's cultural preten-
sions and remains to this day a building encrusted
with all the grandeur of French *amour propre*.

It was the symbolism attached to the opera house
that made it central to Louis Napoléon's Parisian

A drawing of Garnier's plan for the Rue Auber facade of
the Opéra, with the imperial pavilion (now housing the
Bibliothèque de l'Opéra) at the center. (WIKIMEDIA COMMONS)

project. Ever since the seventeenth-century court of the Sun King, Louis XIV, opera and ballet had been a soft-power vehicle of absolutist propaganda. Lavish masque-like entertainments were staged in either the staterooms, stables, or gardens of the palace of Versailles, which oddly lacked its own theater. Sung and danced in elaborately contrived and extravagantly costumed stagings, these shows focused on mythological subjects that allegorically flattered regal virtue and munificence—on occasion, the king himself, an elegant dancer, would make a climactic formal appearance as if providing a blessing.

During the reign of Louis XV (1715–1774), the emphasis of the court shifted to Paris, where under the auspices of the chartered Académie Royale de Musique, the baroque masterpieces of Lully and Rameau (still occasionally revived today) were played in a variety of the capital's theaters open to wealthy members of the public as well as to the aristocratic élite. The Opéra (as the Académie Royale de Musique was generally known) remained itinerant during the Revolutionary and Napoléonic periods, until in 1821 it came to rest in a cramped and inadequate theater in the 9th arrondissement known as the Salle Le Peletier.

By the 1830s, the formal and classical subject matter of the baroque era had fallen radically out of fashion, to be replaced by large-scale dramas, loosely based on historical fact and implicitly endorsing religious tolerance, progressive enlightenment, and a degree of political liberalism. These grand operas, as they were called—such as Rossini's *Guillaume Tell* (1829), Meyerbeer's *Les Huguenots* (1836), and Verdi's *Don Carlos* (1867)—were structured over five acts, always including a ballet sequence in the middle (only tangentially linked to the plots but essential in order to satisfy those in the audience who relished exposure of the female physique), a spectacular processional march, and some strong dramatic or scenic highlight such as a swordfight or conflagration. These works formed the core of the Opéra's repertory: invariably sung in French by French casts,[3] their performances provided a showcase for the nation's artistic riches at their best.[4]

The morally elevated tone that pervaded this business made it appropriate to set before a monarch—enthroned in a royal box, safe from abusive crowds or embarrassing mishaps, he and his courtiers could display themselves graciously, often inviting honored or diplomatic guests to join them in the ritual. Louis Napoléon had none of Queen

Victoria's genuine taste for grand opera (he much preferred the sauce and snap of Jacques Offenbach), but he endured its longueurs in the knowledge that his ceremonial appearances at the Salle Le Peletier would enhance his prestige. So it was a particularly horrible shock when in 1858, a rabid Italian nationalist named Felice Orsini, enraged by France's recent opposition to the unification of his fatherland, threw three powerful homemade bombs at the imperial carriage as it drew up outside the opera house for a performance of *Guillaume Tell.*

Like so many terrorists, Orsini and his accomplices missed their target and ended up slaughtering only innocents. Eight bystanders were killed and 150 wounded in the ensuing carnage. Miraculously, Louis Napoléon and Eugénie escaped injury. Bravely, they continued into the theater and sat stoically through the performance, doubtless shuddering from the shock but determined to send out the right message and stabilize the panic. One significant aftereffect of the episode was to hasten the decision to build an ostentatiously new and commodious opera house, complete with a gated side entrance and covered courtyard that would allow the emperor's carriage secure and exclusive access to the building.

Sculptors and laborers working on the decoration of Garnier's Opéra. (© Beaux-Arts de Paris, Dist. RMN-Grand Palais / image Beaux-arts de Paris)

In 1861 Haussmann identified the appropriate 1.2 hectare site, a brief for the project was published, and a time limit of one month was set for preliminary submissions. Each of the 171 architects entering the competition was asked to submit his plans with the heading of a motto: the winning portfolio quoted a line from the sixteenth-century Italian poet Torquato Tasso—"*Bramo assai, poco spero*" ("I yearn for much, hope for little")—as its tag.

This was the brainwave of thirty-six-year-old Charles Garnier, a rank outsider whose appointment caused a sensation. Born a blacksmith's son in the proletarian Rue Mouffetard, he had risen by his own talents and efforts to be trained at the École des Beaux Arts and to win the prestigious Prix de Rome and make the obligatory grand tour of Italy and Greece. Although he had worked for several years as a civil servant on small municipal projects, he had built nothing in Paris at the time of the competition, and his proposals barely qualified through the first rounds. Yet as the field narrowed, Garnier worked harder and harder on refining his plans, and as more-senior names became hazier and sloppier about details, he became ever more precise.

Eugénie, a reactionary in all matters who had promoted the cause of her favorite architect, Eugène

Viollet-le-Duc, was irritably skeptical when Garnier presented his designs at the Tuileries. "What is this style? It is no style at all—not Ancient Greek, not Louis Seize, not even Louis Quinze!" she snorted. To which Garnier magnificently retorted: "*Ces styles-là ont fait leur temps. C'est du Napoléon III et vous vous plaignez!*" ("Those styles have had their day. This is the style of Napoléon III, and you're complaining about it!").[5]

But both parties in this awkward exchange were right: there is something disconcertingly promiscuous about the design, as well as something idiosyncratically original and even prescient. Although it was to a degree influenced by Victor Louis's chastely elegant 1780s opera house in Bordeaux, in comparison to the relatively austere and academic architectural standards of the Second Empire, its character is extravagantly imaginative—palatial rather than theatrical and more striking in its flamboyantly gilded foyers than in its stage or auditorium. Unusually constructed out of traditional masonry round an iron frame, it fits no stylistic template, mixing elements of Renaissance classicism, mannerist baroque, and ornamental rococo; the architectural historian Gérard Fontaine also believes that in its use of thirty-three varieties of marble, its shimmering mosaics, barbarically vivid colors, and lushly sensuous curves, it heralds the art nouveau of the decadent *fin de siècle*. Some ninety artists contributed to its phantasmagoric interior decoration. This caused much discussion: a silly scandal, whipped up by the tabloid press, was provoked in 1869 when some unidentified prude flung a pot of black ink over a prominent feature of the facade, Jean-Baptiste Carpeaux's exuberantly nude sculpture titled "La Danse."[6]

Because the scheme to build a new opera house was state funded and personally sanctioned by Louis Napoléon, it fell outside Haussmann's jurisdiction, allowing Garnier relatively free rein. Nevertheless, as is inevitable with any project of this scope, he had massive hurdles to surmount from the beginning—for the first six months of the works, eight steam pumps labored round the clock to drain the foundations saturated by a previously unsuspected underground river (later to be mythologized in Gaston Leroux's 1910 tale *The Phantom of the Opera*). Arguments, delays, complications, compromises, and obstacles would result in escalating costs: the budget rose from 29 million to 36 million francs, although Garnier insisted that at 83 francs per cubic meter, this represented excellent value, and the building's longevity and celebrity vindicate him. One stroke of bad luck could have been avoided had they only waited for technology to catch up: the gas pipes that provided the building with its heat and light became redundant within six years of its opening and required expensive replacement with the newly harnessed power of electricity.

Garnier was intensely nervous, whippet-thin, and sickly, but he was buoyed up by a keen sense of humor and an underlying steeliness that came from his working-class origins. For fourteen years, he accepted no other commissions, devoting his life to the creation of what he called "a worldly cathedral of civilisation." Proud as he was of his achievement, he remained disappointed that he never had the time or the money to complete all its finer points. What would enrage him most later in life was the overweening height of buildings on the new avenue of approach from the Louvre, diminishing the impact of his facade at its apex: "I curse the Prefect of the Seine and the developers who have mercilessly shut the Opéra into a huge box." Posterity has not invariably admired a building that the urban sociologist Richard Sennett once described as "an enormous wedding cake sagging under the weight of its decoration,"[7] but Garnier had bequeathed Paris one of the great buildings of the nineteenth century, now as embedded in the cityscape as Nôtre-Dame or the Eiffel Tower.[8]

✦

IN TWO RESPECTS, NEITHER HAUSSMANN nor Louis Napoléon can be justly accused of ulterior motives or personal aggrandizement: both the creation of public parks and the development of the water supply and sewage system were social investments that benefited all Parisians, whatever their class, and still do so today.

Before Haussmann, the Bois de Boulogne was little better than urban wasteland, overgrown and untended since it was first laid out in the era of Louis XIV and the hideout of several less respectable elements of society. Louis Napoléon dreamed of transforming it into something resembling the landscaped elegance of Hyde Park, with its Rotten Row for riders and charming Serpentine pond, but this required a sophistication of landscaping and hydraulics quite beyond the genteel elderly gardener who was then in charge. Haussmann wisely pushed him out and established a new department with the engaging name of the Service de Promenades et Plantations,

One of the many artfully contrived features of the newly landscaped Bois de Boulogne. (Wikimedia Commons)

which he delegated to an ambitious young Jewish civil engineer with whom he had dealt in Bordeaux. This was one of his boldest appointments and perhaps the most fruitful: Jean-Charles Alphand would prove one of Haussmann's happiest collaborators, the two men each perfectly tuned to the other.

The Bois de Boulogne had to be blasted. Its dry, sandy soil needed a new system of irrigation; its undergrowth needed clearing; its paths needed rerouting. The additional demolition of some crumbling redundant walls meant the park could be extended down to the Seine across a flat, barren expanse known as Longchamp that would be transformed into a superb racecourse to rival Ascot or Epsom, replacing the Champ de Mars, better used as a military parade ground. Supervised by Alphand and keenly overseen by the emperor himself—who contributed his own dilettante ideas as to the routes that paths should take—the works were completed between 1854 and 1857 without controversy or obstruction. Interspersing the picturesque bosky glades and cascading waterfalls were charming chalets, restaurants, bandstands, a skating rink, and a theater. Sale of some abutting land for luxury housing and of franchises for the racecourse meant that the project came in at a price that discouraged argument.[9]

The only problem was that the population of the more prosperous west side of Paris was the chief beneficiary. Opening up a similar gift to the more-proletarian areas of the city would prove trickier. An arid and densely forested strip in the East was the obvious choice: originally a hunting park, the Bois de Vincennes had largely been requisitioned by the army in the early nineteenth century. Replicating many of the Bois de Boulogne's pleasure-garden aspects, the Bois de Vincennes covers almost a tenth of the total area of Paris— larger than London's Richmond Park and three times the size of New York's Central Park. But this time there was no convenient source of water to make the desert bloom: dirty heavy industry including a munitions factory had to be bought out at vast cost, and because there was no prospect of offsetting the expense by selling fringes of land for housing development, the total cost would end up being four times that of the Bois de Boulogne.

Lesser novelties that appeared on Alphand's watch include the Parc de Montsouris in the 14th arrondissement, spread over the site of a former stone quarry honeycombed with tunnels and the ossuaries of the ancient catacombs, richly planted in exotic trees and home to a meteorological station; and the pretty Parc Monceau in the 8th arrondissement, celebrated for its golden gates, rococo follies, and a grotto in the English style of Stowe or Stourhead.

Perhaps the most complex challenge was a barren rocky outcrop in the city's Northeast, formerly a place of public execution and a limestone quarry before it became a rubbish dump known as the Buttes-Chaumont. Horse carcasses and sewage had made it a breeding ground for stench, slime, and disease, but Haussmann loved a challenge in the name of public hygiene, and the clearance involved became one of his pet projects. Over a four-year period, 1863–1867, paths were cut into the rock, which had to be reinforced with concrete; thousands of tons of fresh topsoil were imported to cover the surface; and a canal was ingeniously diverted to provide water for the artificial lake, ornamented with a bridge designed by an aspiring young engineer called Gustave Eiffel. The site was crowned with a faux Temple of the Sibyl, inspired by a similar edifice in the gardens of Tivoli's Villa d'Este.

These wonderful parks were part of a greening of central Paris that saw the provision of leafy open space increase from fewer than 20 hectares in 1850 to more than 1,600 by 1870. In addition, the boulevards were planted with resilient horse chestnut and plane trees, and eighteen tranquil garden squares—the Square du Temple in the Marais is one that remains much loved—were tastefully laid out with stylistically unified street furniture, modeled on similar havens that Louis Napoléon had admired in fashionable parts of London. One land grab blots the record: in 1865 Haussmann expropriated 7 hectares (mostly devoted to a tree nursery) of the much-loved Luxembourg Gardens on the Left Bank to extend a crucial traffic thoroughfare, the Rue de l'Abbé de l'Epée (now the Rue Auguste-Comte). The press went apoplectic over this, and huge protests were incited—it was reported that 100,000 irate citizens turned up to jeer as the workers moved in to begin hacking—and no amount of fountains and kiosks lavished on what remained of the parterre could mollify them. But Haussmann got his way, as he invariably did.[10]

⌒◊◊⌒

YET HIS WORK ON THE boulevards and the parks did not give Haussmann as much satisfaction as his achievement underground—projects that related to a kink in his obsessive-compulsive urge to clear Paris of blockages and improve its overall level of hygiene. He made a point of bathing daily (an eccentricity at that time), and it is telling that in his memoirs, Haussmann compared the invisible pipes and sewers of Paris to human organs "whose movement and maintenance serves the life of the body . . . without disturbing its exterior." In his view, cleanliness was not so much next to godliness as its prerequisite.

Louis Napoléon, in contrast, required the wonder of everything he commissioned to show on the surface. As the memoirs make clear, the emperor did not share Haussmann's fascination for the magic of plumbing and drainage. "I am particularly attached to this particular piece of work because it is truly mine," Haussmann boasts. "I did not find it in the programme of the transformation of Paris drawn up by the Emperor and nobody in the world suggested it to me. It is the fruit of my observations, of my keen researches as a young civil servant, and of my mature meditations. It is my own conception."[11] His strategy had two aspects, and because Louis Napoléon did not personally approve either of them, Haussmann had to fight particularly hard to secure the large amount of funding required.

The priority was the capital's water supply. Although there was plenty to go around, the piping and pumping were so inadequate that most of the flow reached only as far as public fountains, whence it was transported and distributed by carriers' carts: fewer than one household in thirty could access it by turning on their own tap. Despite a population that had mushroomed by a third over fifty years, there had been no substantial expansion of Paris's aqueducts or reservoirs in living memory, and the quality of what came through them was bad or even noxious—much of it was drawn from sewage-contaminated areas of the Seine through a canal built by Napoléon Bonaparte, a conduit for cholera and other waterborne diseases.

Being ferried along Paris's new sewers became a popular tourist activity in the late 1860s. (ARCHIVE PHOTOS / GETTY IMAGES)

A proposal suggested transferring all the responsibility to a private contractor who had offered a piecemeal plan to extract more water from the Seine, but Haussmann firmly denied this feeble compromise and went instead over the heads of all the committee protocols and nitpicking ministries to another engineer he had known in Bordeaux. In 1854 Eugène Belgrand became the latest of Haussmann's key collaborators: someone else interested in getting the job done well rather than worrying about the politics behind it. Belgrand's specialties were geology and hydrology; his extraordinary ability to use gravity to channel water would be applied to the ornamental streams, lakes, and cascades of Alphand's parks as well as the much-more-ambitious business of bypassing the Seine and providing Paris, uniquely among major cities, with a system of *eau potable* that ran entirely separately from its system of *eau non potable.*

Haussmann and Belgrand came up with a scheme to collect water into what was then the world's largest reservoir, situated next to the Parc de Montsouris, via a new aqueduct linked to the pure and plentiful springs of the river Dhuys, a tributary of the Marne, about 160 kilometers (100 miles) northeast of Paris in the Aisne region. Although it turned out to be much more of a challenge than anyone had anticipated, embracing a decade of alterations and extensions as well as a big overspend on the budget, it ultimately proved a triumph that brought fresh drinking water even to the outlying suburbs annexed in 1860, as well as vastly increasing the number of households that had direct access.[12]

Sewage was a more intractable but no less important matter. Before Haussmann, many open sewers running down cobbled streets received the contents of the chamber pots; night-soil solids were still gathered in medieval fashion on carts that dumped the excrement into pits in the suburbs. There was only one main collector sewer to take the liquid waste, which was discharged, raw and unhealthy, into the Seine near the Bois de Boulogne—at least until the river swelled in spring and the runnels choked. The narrow tunnels of this ancient warren were notorious. The murderous revolutionary Jean-Paul Marat had hunkered down in one of its obscure corners when fleeing arrest in 1791, and it was here that he may well have contracted the dreadful skin disease that confined him to a bathtub for the rest of his life. The legend of the sewers was further dramatized in a celebrated episode in *Les Misérables,* Victor Hugo's best-selling historical novel of 1862, in the course of which Jean Valjean, heroically bearing Marius's corpse over his shoulders, navigates their horrors in an attempt to evade arrest at the hands of vindictive Inspector Javert.[13]

Haussmann and Belgrand positioned a much bigger waste collector in Asnières, farther from the city center, and in less than five years constructed over 60 kilometers (37 miles) of adjoining new tunnels, complete with a flippered wagon ingeniously designed to flush and clean them. Completed in time for the *Exposition universelle* of 1867, these spacious tunnels had gaslit galleries that became a major tourist attraction, notably visited by both the tsar of Russia and the king of Portugal and considered "so neat and clean that a lady might walk along them . . . without bespattering her skirts." As the newspaper columnist Louis Veuillot proclaimed, perhaps tongue in cheek, "People who have seen everything say that our sewers are possibly the most beautiful thing in the world."[14]

4

PLEASURES OF
THE NEW BABYLON

PARIS S'AMUSE, THEY SAID. PARIS knew how to
have fun, and Parisians could not care less about
politics as long as they could stay at the party. In
the mid-nineteenth century—throughout Europe
an era of primness and caution, nervousness about
revolution and nonconformity—the city thus became a target for the straitlaced, the pious, and
the hypocritical, who regarded it as the equivalent
of Las Vegas, somewhere that no decent person's
morals were safe. "The Vanity Fair of the universe!"
fulminated the Victorian sage Thomas Carlyle, on
the basis of very limited firsthand experience.[1]

But many local pundits and prophets feared that
the city had sold its soul to superficiality: Parisians

are terribly and terminally bored, lamented the controversialist Louis Veuillot in his influential column in *L'Univers;* another pundit, Amédée de Césena, picked up this theme when he wrote that "Parisian society allows everything because it believes in nothing . . . beneath the flowers and diamonds of its ladies, the braid and medals of its gentlemen, lurks a mysterious and fatal poison which gnaws and consumes—boredom."[2] Gustave Flaubert privately thought that Paris was "just completely epileptic, with a madness that springs from excessive stupidity. Our dishonesty has turned us into idiots."[3]

So much for the intellectuals! For everyone else, it was a different story. Through all the dust, scaffolding, and inconvenience thrown up by Haussmann's efforts, Paris offered a ceaseless carnival with something to satisfy all classes and tastes. The biggest parties of all came with the *Expositions universelles* of 1855 and 1867, inspired by the success of London's Crystal Palace Great Exhibition of 1851.

The 1867 iteration would mark the high noon of the Second Empire. Given the highly competitive atmosphere created by the extension of free trade, the focus of the exhibits was more commercial and industrial than it had been a decade earlier—the fine arts were downgraded into an inferior display, and the more-radical painters of the day, Gustave Courbet, age forty-eight, and Edouard Manet, thirty-six, decided to exhibit privately after being rejected officially. Yet despite a near-disastrous opening ceremony in April marred by unopened packing cases, flapping tarpaulins, and acres of spring mud, the result was a triumph, and Haussmann was lavished with medals, titles, and ribbons in consequence. He deserved at least some of them: he and his minions had done an astonishing job of planning, and over the ensuing seven months some nine million visitors passed through the show, including Tsar Alexander II (who narrowly escaped a potshot from a Polish assassin), Bismarck, and the Prince of Wales.

The centerpiece, erected on the Champ de Mars (where the Eiffel Tower now stands), was a Colosseum-shaped Palais de l'Industrie, covering thirty-six acres and painted in brown and gold, inside which forty-two nations competitively presented their prize innovations and achievements. Ominously, the Prussians chose to display a gargantuan steel cannon, built by the mighty Krupp factory, borrowed from its fortifications of the Rhine.[4]

Surrounding the Palais was a park offering all the fun of the fair: photographers' booths, a balloon for hire, an aquarium, restaurants offering exotic cuisines peddling novelties such as caviar and noodles. What caused most amusement were the plasterboard buildings, presented in the manner of a film set, illustrating national architectural styles: Russia offered a facsimile of the tsar's stables, Egypt supplied a miniature temple of the pharaohs, and all things from Japan, newly opened to Europe, became the rage. Much derided was a half-timbered "English cottage" with high brick chimneys that was thought to resemble nothing so much as the gingerbread house of Hansel and Gretel: it contained unprepossessing displays of factory pottery from Stoke-on-Trent.[5]

Yet it was not only in exhibition years that international tourism boomed. In consequence of the Free Trade treaty of 1860, passports between Britain and France were not required, and since the journey from London Bridge to the Gare du Nord via the Folkestone boat train took only some ten hours, short holidays and even long weekend breaks were both feasible and popular. Lavish accommodation was provided by the likes of the Péreire Brothers' seven-hundred-room Grand Hôtel on the Boulevard des Capucines, which offered the innovations of a hydraulic "lifting machine . . . raising clients

The interior of the great salle that formed the centerpiece of the magnificent *Exposition universelle* of 1867. (© Musée d'Orsay, Dist. RMN-Grand Palais / Patrice Schmidt)

to their floor" and electric bells—albeit, according to the Baedeker Guide, "few private w.c.s" and a shortage of "quiet, prompt attendance." The aristocracy preferred the more select and venerable

Hôtel Meurice in the Rue de Rivoli, whereas Yankees made for the Hôtel de Calais in the Rue Neuve des Capucines, which served fish balls and buckwheat cakes with maple syrup for breakfast and stood reassuringly next door to the American bank.

Restaurants, then as now, were ubiquitous, ranging from the top-end Véfour, Café Riche, and Trois Frères Provençaux abutting the Palais-Royal, to the modestly respectable chains of Monsieur Duval's *cremeries* (dairies) and *bouillons* (soup kitchens) with their *prix fixe* menus and respectable waitresses dressed like nuns, to self-service canteens such as the warehouse La Californie, owned by an enterprising butcher who claimed to provide 18,000 plates of rabbit stew daily for workingmen. More than 20,000 cafés offered not only beverages and simple fare but also France's most popular intoxicant—the "green fairy" liqueur of absinthe, distilled from aniseed and imported from Algeria—as well as the relaxation of newspapers, billiards, chess, and card games. The Boulevard des Italiens was a favored resort: in the afternoon, fashionable folk foregathered at Tortoni, which sold fabulous ice cream or a glass of Madeira with patisserie; after the theater or opera, everyone moved to the Café Anglais, which was open all night. Male conviviality was the keynote in such places; ladies had to be accompanied in order to remain unmolested. Red as well as white wine, oddly, was normally drunk diluted with seltzer.[6]

Entertainment was similarly pitched at everything from grand opera or classic drama at the Comédie-Française (where an eighteen-year-old ingenue called Sarah Bernhardt, of uncertain parentage, made her nervous debut in 1862) through the piquant hit operettas of Offenbach at the Bouffes-Parisiens on the Rue Monsigny. Those in search of something earthier made for bustling *cafés-chantants* such as L'Alcazar on the Rue du Faubourg Poissonnière—where cabaret singers such as the uninhibitedly vulgar Theresa offered coarse popular songs that could turn scandalously smutty and satirical—or to the *bals publics*, dance halls in which genteel polkas and waltzes licensed flirtation and spooning. The lower-class suburban dives did not bother with the niceties of courtship: after midnight, the raucous can-can ruled. Today it is envisaged only in its latter-day sanitized form, in which a cheerfully whooping chorus line reveals nothing more than a frothing mass of white petticoats and knickers, but in its more authentic original incarnation it was a mating ritual in which the women wore nothing underneath their skirts and their high kicks were an invitation to orgy. The police kept close watch on premises where this sort of behavior was displayed, both as overt guardians of public decency and as covert spies on anyone exploiting the crowd's excitement to foment seditious political views.[7]

༺ঌ৩༻

PARIS WAS ALSO EUROPE'S MARKETPLACE—no other city could match the splendor and extent of its shopping opportunities. *Grands magasins* such as Au Bon Marché, precursor of the modern department store on the Rue de Sèvres, contained treasure troves of drapery, haberdashery, furniture, and household goods over several floors: a job behind the counter in such an emporium was the height of a working-class girl's professional aspirations, even though the discipline and etiquette required were positively militaristic in their rigidity. Marketing tactics adopted by Au Bon Marché's mastermind, Aristide Boucicaut (and subsequently much imitated), included elaborate window displays, full-page advertisements in the press, a shop layout that enticed the gullible from one purchase to the next,

Paris s'amuse: a Second Empire banquet. (ROGER VIOLLET / TOPFOTO)

low prices based on high turnover, the guarantee of "total satisfaction" on the basis of a liberal exchange or return policy, and mail-order facilities. Out on the pavements, more-furtive transactions took place as hucksters whisperingly hawked forbidden books and obscene photographs, and pimps and "flower girl" prostitutes cruised for customers.

Because syphilis was rightly perceived to be at least as much of a menace to public health as cholera or typhoid, intense official efforts were made to control prostitution. Brothels (many of them displaced from the rookeries of the Île de la Cité by Haussmann's plans) and individual operators were required to register themselves with the police and conform to a stern code of regulation that strictly limited the field and decreed regular submission to humiliatingly intimate physical inspections, with fines, imprisonment, and disqualifications waiting for those who breached their license. Not surprisingly, many preferred to take the risk of playing outside a heavy-handed system that offered no advantages or protection, and the numbers of these *insoumises* or *non-inscrites* (unregistered) ran so high that "respectable" women going innocently about their daily business struggled to distinguish themselves and avoid embarrassing advances.

The facade of Au Bon Marché, the department store that created a new model for up-market shopping. (ROGER VIOLLET/GETTY IMAGES)

The police reckoned that something in the range of 30,000 prostitutes were out and about. "One doesn't know nowadays if it's honest women who are dressed like whores or whores who are dressed like honest women," commented Flaubert's friend

Maxime du Camp wryly, as Paris became known as a city of "universal prostitution."[8]

> The consequent pastime of speculating who might be up for hire was one that kept the Parisian male in a constant priapic itch. Yet the longer-term price for succumbing to the temptation to scratch was high: over 50,000 cases of venereal disease were recorded in Paris per annum, with only the partially effective and thoroughly nasty mercury and potassium iodide available as treatment.[9]

More-romantic types could dream, too. Even if a girl was not to be bought for an hour or a night, was she perhaps a *grisette* (one happy to sleep with a boyfriend, like Mimi in *La Bohème*) or a *lorette* (willing to adopt an older man as her protector, like Musetta in *La Bohème*)? In the realm of fable and rumor there also dwelt the courtesans or *grandes horizontales*, an élite of dangerous sirens who could cost a man a small fortune in diamonds in return for the glimpse of a breast or a kiss of a foot. "All my wishes have come to heel, like tame dogs," crowed the most notorious of them all, Esther Lachmann, known to gossipers as La Païva, a Polish-Jewish weaver's daughter who made her way from wealthy lovers in Berlin, Vienna, London, and Istanbul to Paris, where she came to roost in a monstrously vulgar mansion on the Champs Elysées, constructed and fitted out on millions milked from industrialist Guido Henckel von Donnersmarck, twelve years her junior, who finally became her husband. Hard as nails and not wildly beautiful, Lachmann aspired to mix in sophisticated literary circles. According to the mesmerized Goncourt brothers, invited to one of her ludicrously grand dinners, she was "*sotte mais pas bête*" ("witless but nobody's fool").[10]

⌇

PARIS S'AMUSE, LIKE NOWHERE ELSE did. But the other side of the coin was *Paris s'ennuie:* a deep and corrosive melancholy that lurked behind the hectic pursuit of sensual satisfaction and the revolving doors of fashion and novelty. Everybody with any intelligence felt the panic, the emptiness, the banality of it all. In his satire *Notes sur Paris: La Vie et opinions de Monsieur Frederic-Thomas Graindorge,* published in 1867, Hippolyte Taine analyzed the phenomenon perceptively: once the capital's typical young man of mode had thought about "his toilet, his furnishings, his little image of himself, he has come to the end of his ideas."[11] A variety of this self-absorption was also the malaise among the educated and cultured. Aesthetic purists such as Gustave Flaubert and Charles Baudelaire were cynical reactionaries in their political stance: both disliked Parisian life, but they did not so much hate or oppose the Second Empire as despise it to the point of ignoring it. Their substitute for socialism or republicanism was the sort of cosmically irritable personal gloom that Baudelaire romanticized as "spleen." "*Paris change,*" he reflected in his poem "Le Cygne" ("The Swan"), "*mais rien dans mon mélancolie/n'a bougé*" ("Paris changes, but nothing in my melancholy has moved").

Others had a chilly intuition of greater disaster: the Goncourt brothers, loyal Parisians to the core, wrote in their jointly composed diary in 1869 that "all the trees in Paris are starting to die. . . . Ancient nature is disappearing. She leaves a land poisoned by civilization."[12] It may not have been true—Haussmann is said to have doubled the city's public foliage—but it felt as though it was.

How much of this angst was the effect of Haussmann's project? It was certainly exhausting for ordinary folk to live in a city in an ongoing state of violent physical flux—some compared it to a constant earthquake—in which the ax might fall very fast without redress. Expropriations took place with astonishing speed, as Felix Whitehurst, the foppish correspondent for the *Daily Telegraph*, only slightly caricatured:

> Man in cocked hat calls and leaves paper (this is Monday). On Wednesday he returns with two other devils worse than himself, and not only gives you notice to quit, but fixes the day and the hour; and as the last box leaves the tenement one workman pulls down the door and the inspector makes a *bureau des démolitions* of the lodge from which your faithful concierge handed you—sometimes—your letters. You pass by on the Saturday, and all is a blank. Six grey Normandy horses, and four men much addicted to bad language, are laying the first stone of the rue Champignon, late rue de Chêne.[13]

The spectacle of change was bizarre, surreal, enervating. Anyone wanting to admire the new Paris, wrote the columnist Victor Fournel,

> Will jostle labourers hacking at a hovel or a palace with a pickaxe or hitched to a rope and shouting

as they pull down a side of wall which crumbles into a whirl of dust . . . will encounter rows of houses decapitated, disemboweled, divided, sinking into holes . . . must at every step make a detour along the middle of the road heeding the cries of Watch out!; must avoid the piles of rubble or mortar at his feet. To one's left and right are carts, horses, builders whitened with plaster dust; over one's head, tiles or distemper rains down; and everywhere one hears that infernal orchestra of tools cutting stone, the creaking of cranes and the hoarse cussing of peasants.[14]

Haussmann is often presented as a hard-nosed vandal who ruthlessly knocked down everything that stood in his way. This is not altogether fair: yes, he demolished some beautiful (but at that time unloved and decrepit) town mansions in Saint-Germain that would now be listed and sacrosanct, but only with the Île de la Cité was he absolutely brutal—devastating an entire community, albeit one that was a warren of thieves, hopelessly dilapidated, and infested with disease.

Elsewhere, despite his obsessive determination to clean up and regularize, he accepted that some monuments needed not only preservation but also conservation, and he duly commissioned a scholarly survey of old Paris aimed at mapping and photographing all the streets and areas that were being replaced.[15] Haussmann also ordered in 1866 the purchase of the Marais mansion of the great seventeenth-century *belle-lettriste* Madame de Sévigné: this became the Musée Carnavalet, which continues today to offer a magnificent pageant of the city's past.

But attachment to place is not an emotion that can easily be eradicated, and ever since Victor Hugo had romanticized the moldering maze of the medieval city in his 1831 novel *Nôtre-Dame de Paris,* the "authentic atmosphere" of the backstreets had been sentimentalized—even if the harsh reality was only fetid urban swamps such as the Carré Saint Martin, behind the Rue de Rivoli, where the pathetically destitute slept on benches, pickled by cheap hooch and kept alive by what they could beg or a few *sous* earned from machine turning.

Some who owed their advancement to the regime rushed to Haussmann's defense, one such being the favored newspaper hack Amédée de Césena, who in his pamphlet *Le nouveau Paris* acknowledged that the wide boulevards were a protection against backstreet rioting and took a brisk line: "I am as fond of memories attached to old buildings as anyone else, but I do not understand how one can prefer narrow and twisting alleys to wide and regular streets, or decrepit and unhealthy dwelling to elegant and salubrious ones."[16]

More common was a posture of breast-beating Old Testament lamentation, as typified by Louis Veuillot in *Les Odeurs de Paris:* "City without a past, full of spirits without memories, of hearts without tears, of souls without love! City of uprooted multitudes!" and so forth, the idea being that it was not just a physical landscape that was being destroyed but a spiritual one too. The journalist and politician Jules Ferry similarly bemoaned "with eyes full of tears for the old Paris, the Paris of Voltaire, of Desmoulins, of 1830 and 1848" in contrast to "the triumphant vulgarity, the appalling materialism that we will bequeath our descendants."[17]

Charles Garnier's critique of 1869 had a more visionary quality:

I dream of the day when tawny shades of gold will spangle our city's monuments and buildings. We will then stop building big straight streets that although beautiful, are as cold and stiff as a dowager. Our streets will become less rigid and, without hurting anyone, a man will be able to build his house as he pleases, without worrying whether or not it fits in with his neighbour's. Cornices will shine with the colours of eternity; gold friezes will sparkle on facades, monuments will be decorated in marble and enamel, and mosaics will make the city vibrate with colour. This will not be meretricious. It will be true opulence. Once people have become accustomed to the city's marvellous, dazzling nuances, they will demand that our clothes be redesigned and brightened up as well, and the entire city will be harmoniously bathed in silks and gold. . . . But alas I look around and see a sombre grey sky, renovated houses and dark shadows trudging along the endless boulevards. In short, I see Paris as it really is![18]

Perhaps the most interesting contemporary assessment is that of Victor Fournel, whose *Paris nouveau et Paris futur* was published in 1865. He admitted the gains of "a certain grandiose aspect essential to the character of a great capital city . . . air, light and spaciousness. Unhealthy quarters have been cleansed, monuments exposed and a canny strategic network traced around the city." But if only it had stopped there, he continued. Instead,

Haussmann had ended up becoming "the Attila of the straight line," and Paris had lost "the picturesque, the variety, the unexpected, the charm of discovery which made a stroll across the older Paris a voyage of exploration across worlds always fresh and unknown, this multi-faceted and living physiognomy that gave unique traits to each area of the city as though they were human faces." Now what dominated was a monotonously rectilinear magnificence that removed "bumps, angles, and contours" in order to substitute "a new white city that made cat litter out of its most curious or sacred memories; a city of shops and cafés . . . a city of pomp, destined to become one great big hotel for foreign tourists."[19]

Such litanies have continued unabated into the twenty-first century, where a culture that fetishizes the old and crumbling battles with the bulldozing capitalist insistence on maximizing its efficiency. It is piquant to read a modern American essayist, Rebecca Solnit, mourning the demise of Haussmann's Paris in precisely the terms that the nostalgics had been using a century earlier about the streets that were being demolished in the name of progress:

The vast void on the Right Bank was the site where the great Les Halles markets had recently been eradicated . . . traffic lights would come to the crooked old streets of the Latin Quarter and illuminated plastic signs for fast food would mar the old walls . . . , the Tuileries' and Luxembourg's metal chairs with their spiral arms and perforated circular seats (in much the same aesthetic vein as the pissoirs) would be replaced by more rectilinear and less beautiful chairs painted the same green.[20]

Plus ça change.

5

HAUSSMANN'S DOWNFALL

BOTH THE GRANDEUR OF TRAGEDY and an element of dismal banality color Haussmann's fate— he went out with his head held high but his tail between his legs, and although he never suffered public humiliation, the remainder of his life would be spent in the shadows. From the mid-1860s he was sliding unstoppably down the slippery slope of politics, and despite the public's gratitude for the improvements in the water supply, sewers, and parks, his final assault on the shortcomings of Paris's public hygiene system proved his one outright failure.

The disposal of human corpses would remain controversial in France until the 1960s, when the Second Vatican Council mitigated the problem by sanctioning cremation for Catholics for the first time. But in Second Empire Paris, burial was still the rule, with all its attendant health hazards. After hundreds of years, the churchyards were almost full, and the cemeteries of Père Lachaise, Montparnasse, and Montmartre, opened between 1804 and 1825, soon would be.

Attacking this problem, Haussmann overstepped the mark. Presciently calculating the future population of the city and supported by a report chaired by Belgrand pointing to the contamination of the water supply by seepage from the cemeteries (not to mention air dense with the stench of putrid corpses), he secretly came up with the idea of establishing a vast municipal necropolis on an empty plain some 23 kilometers (14 miles) north of Paris at Méry-sur-Oise—a project inspired by Brookwood Cemetery, near Woking in Surrey, which opened in 1854.[1]

Anticipating a frenzy of speculation the moment the plan was made public, he cunningly but not illegally established a company that cheaply bought up all the required land—some five hundred hectares—without anyone knowing what he intended doing with it. His view was that Paris had thus secured itself a bargain, but when the story emerged in 1867, the press decided otherwise and drew its knives: for the pundits, this was a plot typical of Haussmann's megalomaniac tendency to act without due process, and even if it was not strictly corrupt, it didn't look right. In *Le Correspondant*, Victor Fournel fulminated that "the expropriation of the living is being followed by the expropriation of the dead and the deportation of corpses, centralized in a necropolis which will be the Botany Bay of deceased Parisians." So with rumors of death trains and ghost roads giving everyone the shivers, the plan faltered, and the status quo held.[2]

The scandal, such as it was, was one that Haussmann could weather; there was no smoking gun or any question that he had in any way profited personally from the land deal. His nemesis would be Jules Ferry, a campaigning journalist (and subsequently a government minister) who in 1868 assembled a series of his newspaper articles in a pamphlet titled *Les Comptes fantastiques d'Haussmann* (*Haussmann's Fantastic Accounts*), a glancing pun on *Les Contes fantastiques d'Hoffmann,* a popular collection of "magical realism" tales by the German novelist E. T. A. Hoffmann, subsequently adopted as the title of an opera by Offenbach.[3]

Not all that Ferry said was revelatory: for several years there had been mutterings of complaint, not only on the aesthetic and sentimental grounds previously discussed but also because of the sense that the redevelopment excessively favored the wealthy at the expense of deprived suburbs and working-class quarters. Outsiders noticed that the government's budget for Paris had risen ten times over that allotted to the rest of the country. For Parisians themselves, there was also the sheer daily irritation of living in a city constantly in upheaval thanks to an endless succession of dusty, noisy, obstructive building sites. Haussmann's schemes were no longer making improvements necessary or beneficial to the public good, so people said; they were simply a form of showing off and an opportunity for the rich to make more money for themselves.

For most of his career in Paris, Haussmann had easily shrugged off criticism or opposition. Restrictions on freedom of assembly and speech combined with press censorship meant that mass dissent could have little effect. In any case, only people directly affected by expropriation or demolition would be likely to object, and the great majority of them could be mollified with generous compensation terms. Only when he shaved some acres off the Jardin de Luxembourg in order to widen what is now the Rue Auguste-Comte did his activities come anywhere near causing outright mass protest. The era lacked powerfully organized and funded lobbies such as the National Trust, which in today's England can lobby against overweening government decisions, nor the did the law offer historical buildings any general protection.

But the liberalizations of the mid-1860s had opened the floodgates on widespread, pent-up irritation, and Ferry's critique homed in on the aspect of Haussmann's conduct that played out least well at a time when France was tentatively liberalizing and extending democracy: his unaccountability. Only the emperor seemed to be able to inhibit him, let alone control him; with Louis Napoléon's blessing, he seemed to do pretty much what he liked, and his inborn arrogance had long curdled dangerously into complacence. Without reference to anybody else, he had borrowed hundreds of millions of francs to finance his schemes, debts for which the city then became liable, and laundered them through a fund that he alone controlled. The result was that the city's overall debt had increased in seventeen years from 163 million francs to 2,500 million francs, with interest consuming nearly half of the annual budget.

Ferry's pamphlet pointed the finger in a tirade that was as dramatically forceful and rhetorically

Haussmann's Paris embraced all manner of improvements to its public spaces and hygiene—not least the institution of these picturesque urinals. (Roger Viollet / Topfoto)

powerful as Emile Zola's *"J'accuse"* broadside would be a generation later when Alfred Dreyfus was maliciously convicted of treason:

> We accuse him of having sacrificed the future to his caprices and vainglory; we accuse him of having devoured the inheritance of future generations in works of doubtful or transient utility; we accuse him, of having led us, at a gallop, to the brink of catastrophe. The city has borrowed 398 million francs that it can't repay. That's all. How can 398 million francs have been borrowed without the legislature having had some say in it? Is the city of Paris in control of its affairs, or are they by any chance out of its control?[4]

Ferry's grenade exploded, spreading a scalding debate in its wake, fanned by gossip about Haussmann's long-suffering wife and about his mistresses, a nonentity in the corps de ballet and an operetta soprano. There was nastier stuff as well, such as the baseless rumor that Haussmann had procured his nubile daughter Fanny-Valentine for the emperor's pleasure.[5]

Haussmann would have thought it beneath him to refute such tittle-tattle. Throughout 1869 he defended himself from the fallout with a cool Olympian dignity that further enraged his opponents:

> The service to which I have, for the last sixteen years, subordinated my own interests, personal tastes, my old friendships, even the joys of family life, constitute a capital of honour that I have amassed with jealous care, because this capital will be the clearest part of the heritage that my children will have from me.[6]

In other words, say what you like, but his hands were clean; there had been no dirty deals or backhanders on his watch, and beyond his salary, expenses, and status, he had not profited materially from his deals and operations. In other circumstances he might have survived by allowing some sleight of an accountant's hand to change the way in which the debt was managed. But in the context of reforms leading to open parliamentary discussion, a freer press, a relaxation on the ban on public meetings, and the strengthening of various checks and balances, all of which reduced Louis Napoléon's influence, he was exposed and isolated.

Haussmann had become a political liability, but he remained intransigent to the point of self-destructive myopia: he refused to compromise by submitting to the authority of a council, he would not even sit on such a body, and he certainly would not quietly resign. However, the new government was adamant that the price for his bulldozing efficiency was too high and that he would have to be sacrificed. Always a loner in government, he had few allies and only grudging admirers. Nobody liked him enough to feel moved to argue his case, and so in January 1870 the emperor was forced to dismiss him formally, in the course of a two-hour private meeting of which no record remains.

The following day an announcement appeared in the *Bulletin quotidien de la Cour* (the Court Circular) to the effect that Haussmann had been relieved of his duties as prefect of the Seine to be replaced by the prefect of the Rhône, Henri Chevreau. Haussmann was clearing out his office when, owing to an administrative muddle, he received an official letter inviting the prefect of the Seine to a grand ceremony inaugurating the new parliament—it was intended for Chevreau, of course, but Haussmann decided to interpret it as his by right. Wearing his full uniform and panoply of medals, he and his retinue processed in an ostentatious cortege of carriages through the city he had transformed. Arriving at the reception, he made a pompous entrance to the discomfiture of his deadliest enemies and, amid much florid bowing and insincere compliments, presented his staff to the ministers who had engineered his dismissal. It was a gesture replete with the contemptuous arrogance that had made him so disliked.[7]

Now sixty-one, Haussmann withdrew to his estate near Nice. A few months later, he had another conversation with Louis Napoléon about his possible return to government in another capacity, but nothing came of their discussion. Perhaps feeling that he could not replicate his Parisian achievements, he also turned down offers to mastermind the bigger urban picture for Rome and Istanbul. But he would not be idle. Instead, he sat for some years on the board of the merchant bank Crédit mobilier—reconstituted after the insolvency of its buccaneering founding fathers the Péreire brothers, whose openhanded loans had financed so much activity during the Second Empire—and became senatorial deputy for Corsica, where he was instrumental in pushing through a typically bold plan for a railway cutting through mountainous terrain across the island from Bastia to Ajaccio. He would eventually die in 1891 at the age of eighty-one and was buried in the Parisian cemetery of Père Lachaise.

Such was the resentment that his name had continued to provoke that not a single representative of the city council attended his funeral. Yet, even more justifiably than the great baroque architect of London, Sir Christopher Wren, he could claim as his epitaph *Si monumentum requiris, circumspice* (If you want a memorial to me, just look around).[8]

The news that he had been dismissed was received with both relief and consternation—being rid of this overweening satrap might be a boon, but what would be the fate of projects such as Charles Garnier's opera house that were well down the line but not yet near completion? Felix Whitehurst was one of many who posed that question and naively changed their tune to suggest that Haussmann's departure would be regretted:

> Who on earth can finish the elaborate—I do not even say wise—conceptions of Baron Haussmann, except the Baron himself? Now you cannot leave Paris half unfinished; and that is really what will be the result. That Baron Haussmann should never have come into office is an opinion we can understand, and had he not, the fact perhaps would perhaps have been a saving to Paris; but then we must admit that the new Paris which

we all so much admire would not have existed.
The old narrow streets . . . would have remained
to this day. We should have had no Boulevards,
useful as they are politically as well as socially; for
no great riot can ever rage in Paris now that we
have wide streets. . . . It appears to me, I confess,
that M. Haussmann is a real loss to Paris. He is a
man who has worked very hard, been very much
abused, and yet has done all that was required of
him, and done it nobly. His successor may be very
good; but how can he terminate the great works
which Baron Haussmann began?[9]

The longer-term answer, as we shall see, was that
the wheels of Haussmannization (as the pundits
now dubbed it) would prove unstoppable and would
become a force much bigger than Haussmann himself. Meanwhile, however, events would overtake
France with astonishing speed and rewrite its political agenda: the question was no longer how Paris
would look but on what terms it would survive at all.

6

THE END OF
THE SECOND EMPIRE

HISTORIANS STILL STRUGGLE TO ASSESS Louis Napoléon fairly. No statues of him were erected after his death, and he was unfairly trivialized by unverified gossip about his extramarital dalliances; subsequently, his lack of glamour and swagger or even personality means that he has never been mythologized in posterity's imagination. Even today, France remains unsure whether to celebrate or excoriate his memory: unlike his more forceful and charismatic uncle, who retains a heroic aura despite far more despotic proclivities, he is a figure hard to hate but impossible to love.

Cunning and calculating rather than cruel or vindictive, he was politically astute in his adoption of a benevolent public pose that was sometimes pompous but never overtly aggressive or authoritarian. He also appears to have had a clear and consistent vision of what France wanted and needed. He was always secretive by nature, and something about him remained inscrutable and indefinable; perhaps that was one of his subtle strengths. Did he have principles? Nobody could tell: perhaps the bottom line was merely his own survival and the inheritance of his son, Louis.

What is undoubtedly true is that the coup he staged in 1851 stabilized a nation that had been combustible and discontented as well as unproductive and that his cool chicanery and firm grip on administration resulted in an increase in France's material prosperity—nowhere more so than in Paris, which boomed under the Haussmann dispensation. But surveying the country and the period as a whole, it is evident that sustained growth, high productivity, low unemployment, and rising wages and living standards—those holy grails of modern economies—were all achieved, stimulated by aggressive state investment (particularly in the railway network) and by an extension of free trade.

What is also incontrovertible is that for the lower echelons of society, the chances of bettering their lot and moving up the ladder were limited: the very poor remained very poor, even if they were employed. Those who remained in the city center were badly hit by the rise in rents and crowded their families ever more tightly into the attics, basements, hallways, and stairwells of buildings that Haussmann had yet to condemn. Most of the new labor force was based in shanty suburbs. In his study *Paris, Capital of Modernity,* David Harvey assembles a composite picture:

A recent immigrant from Lorraine in 1865 rents, with his wife and two children, two minuscule rooms in Belleville, towards the periphery of Paris. He leaves every morning at five o'clock, armed with a crust of bread and walks four miles to the center, where he works fourteen hours a day in a button factory. After the rent is paid, his regular wage leaves him fr. 1 a day (bread costs fr. 0.37 a kilo), so he brings home piecework for his wife, who works long hours at home for almost nothing. "To live, for a labourer, is not to die" was a saying of the time.[1]

An employee had no recourse to law: trade unions were banned until 1865; industry was dirty, dangerous, and unregulated; and the rates of respiratory disease and workplace accidents were horrendously high. Do the work, get the money on offer, and like it or lump it represented the extent of the moral compass. For uneducated women in Paris, there was even less hope, even though they formed an estimated one-third of the workforce. Those who had to care for the young or the aged had only the piecework option—dreadfully repetitive and mindless—that Harvey indicates; single girls without children could go into domestic service, with a privileged few becoming shop assistants or waitresses, but the only other possibilities were washing or sewing and the slippery slope that ended for thousands in prostitution. If charity was a partial safety net, there were invariably Catholic strings attached to its beneficence. Novels such as Emile Zola's *L'Assommoir* (1877) confront this situation: scrupulously researched and written with hindsight from an ideological and sociological agenda, they scarcely dramatize the bleakness of this landscape.

In only one important area of social policy did the Second Empire achieve anything that substantially affected the lot of the downtrodden: state education. In 1860 Louis Napoléon began working at his leisure on a biography of Julius Caesar, a figure who for obvious reasons obsessed him. In the course of his research he consulted Victor Duruy, a distinguished classical scholar and teacher at the élite Lycée Henri IV who in the 1840s had published a marvelously vivid and best-selling history of the Romans. The dashingly handsome son of a factory worker, Duruy was a true meritocrat of a reformist and anticlerical persuasion. He was no champion of imperial authoritarianism, but Louis Napoléon, strange and unpredictable man that he was, took a shine to him and in 1863, without consulting him or anyone else, appointed him minister for public instruction. Duruy was horrified at first but accepted the challenge on the understanding that he would be given a free hand in rolling back what he considered to be the baneful influence of the church over the schooling of the impressionable young.

Louis Napoléon agreed and was as good as his word, but things would still not be easy for Duruy: every reform that he wanted to make was vigorously opposed by the Catholic establishment. What he achieved over six years in office in the face of low standards and widespread illiteracy (20 percent of Paris's population could not sign their names; nationwide, the figure was over 50 percent) was nevertheless remarkable, embracing a shake-up of teacher training, legislation that for the first time made primary education compulsory for girls, and the extension of the curriculum to provide for the study of modern history and living languages, as well as the introduction of technical and vocational classes for those who could usefully profit from them. His goals of enforcing compulsory secondary schooling for girls and making all state education free and secular were ahead of his time and would not be realized for another generation. But Victor Duruy must rank as one of the true heroes of the age, and Louis Napoléon should be given credit for empowering him.[2]

Conservative though it may have been in its politics, Louis Napoléon's regime was not skeptical of the liberal ideals of progress or discouraging of enterprise or innovation—far from it, and French industry during this period would be every bit as energized and productive as those of its rivals in England and Germany. Technological advances included the development of aluminum, margarine, color photography, the dry-cell battery, the pneumatic drill, pasteurization, and the refrigerator. Most strikingly visible on the streets was the velocipede, a prototype of the pedal bicycle made of wood with metal wheels from a design pioneered by the Parisian blacksmith Pierre Michaux. It was

The bone-shaking velocipede, a crude early form of bicycle that briefly became a fashionable craze until a more sophisticated and comfortable model with rubber tires superseded it. (Granger Images / Bridgeman Images)

hopelessly uncomfortable to ride until the late 1860s, when the innovation of solid rubber tires reduced the bone-shaking bumps, and suddenly the machine became all the rage.[3]

"Vélocipèdes to the front!" proclaimed Felix Whitehurst, who foresaw the modern cycle lane. "There are private riding schools most aristocratically attended—Lords, Dukes and Princes ... [and] very soon I expect to see in the Bois [de Boulogne] an '*avenue réservée aux vélocipèdes*' and that which is now the reserved ride of cavaliers deserted." A magazine devoted to the sport was published, in which readers learned that a 130-kilometer (80-mile) road race from Paris to Rouen had been won in 10 hours 40 minutes and that the prince impérial, Louis Napoléon's heir, had become a devotee as a result of a thirteenth-birthday gift from his decidedly progressive and modish aunt Princess Mathilde Bonaparte. More significantly, anticipating the time when the velocipede would mutate into a standard mode of transport rather than a rich man's plaything, Whitehurst noted the sight of men disdaining the queues for the omnibus and cycling across Paris to work.[4]

⌒⌒

EVER SINCE PRUSSIA UNDER BISMARCK had defeated the Austrians in 1866 at the Battle of Sadowa—thus consolidating its hold over the German Reich and tipping the European balance of power by neutering France's putative ally in Vienna—it had been evident in diplomatic circles that France and Prussia would eventually come to blows. Were both sides spoiling for a fight? The

French army was ill prepared for such a showdown, fearfully pleased with itself, poorly equipped, and weak in strategy. Its armaments were outdated or ineffectual—the faith invested in a secretly developed early form of machine gun, the rapidly firing *mitrailleuse,* would prove unjustified by its performance in the field—and little attention had been paid to the new idea that troops could usefully be transported by railway. The ranks were depleted, out of fear that conscripted troops might turn mutinous. The science of war, so meticulously studied by the Prussians, was considered crass and even vulgar. Senior officers were imbued by the elitist military academies with an archaic ethos of derring-do and chivalry. "*On se débrouille*" ("We'll muddle through somehow or other") was the generals' shruggingly insouciant watchword.[5]

As the issue of war crept inexorably to the top of the agenda, the Empire's domestic prospects were uncertain. Facing an increasing rumble of opposition from both republican tendencies and those who wanted a restoration of the monarchy, Louis Napoléon had decided that the best course was to yield some outlying ground in order to maintain his hold on the center. Trusting in the loyalty of the electorate to endorse him, he cautiously permitted democratic liberties and relaxed censorship. These gestures—for that is how they were regarded—did not altogether pay off. An open election in 1869, devoid of the intimidation, gerrymandering, and "irregularities" that had previously swung the vote heavily in the Empire's favor, returned the government to power but with a substantially reduced majority. With the conciliatory reformist Emile Ollivier as the new prime minister, Louis Napoléon extended parliamentary powers and prerogatives further and inaugurated what was labeled the "Liberal Empire." For the right this went too far, for the left not far enough. A crisis occurred in January 1870 when Louis Napoléon's black sheep of a cousin, Prince Pierre Bonaparte, shot and killed a widely read republican journalist, Victor Noir, after a trivial argument. Noir's funeral turned into an angry political rally said to have been 200,000 strong, and when after a decidedly irregular trial Pierre Bonaparte was acquitted—on the dubious grounds that he had been provoked—the left's fury was dry tinder.

At a plebiscite held shortly afterward, Louis Napoléon held on impressively with 82 percent of the vote: for most of the French, the Empire continued to represent stability and employment. The question was how Louis Napoléon and his new liberal regime could strengthen their hand, and the only answer to that was to defeat an external enemy—preferably through a stunning diplomatic victory, otherwise by a military campaign.

The emperor's prestige in this department was not high. French meddling in the complexities of Italian nationalism had antagonized other European powers, even if it resulted in the transfer of Nice and Savoy from Piedmont. A subsequent intervention in Mexico brought no benefits, however—on the contrary, it was an unmitigated disaster. In a misguided effort to reestablish a power and trade base in the Americas, Louis Napoléon had intervened in this weakly governed country and sponsored a revival of the Mexican monarchy with Archduke Maximilian of Austria as a puppet emperor. A gentle, charming, and well-meaning progressive, Maximilian nevertheless fell foul of the native republicans and their allies in the United States. Pressure from the White House led Louis Napoléon to withdraw protective French troops, leaving Maximilian powerless. Staunchly refusing to abandon his followers, he continued to defend his regime until the collapse of a siege led to his arrest by the republicans. Despite huge international protest and pleas for clemency, he was eventually shot by firing squad—an event that profoundly shocked France and became a scene subsequently painted by Manet. The French Parliament, newly licensed to speak its mind, did so vehemently. "There is not a single mistake left to make!" thundered Adolphe Thiers, an influential and outspoken critic of Louis Napoléon.[6] But Thiers was wrong: what happened next would be an even greater misjudgment that played into the hands of the mighty Prussian Chancellor Otto von Bismarck and his ambition to unite all the German states in one nation under his control.

When the king of Spain died without an heir, Prussia decided to try its luck by proposing that someone from its own royal dynasty, the Hohenzollern, should assume the throne. Behind this bizarre notion was Bismarck's conviction that France had gotten too big for its European boots. He was enraged by Louis Napoléon's support for the Polish nationalism that threatened to destabilize Prussia's eastern border and felt justified in seeking recompense for Louis Napoléon's land grab of Nice and Savoy in 1860 after the Italian war of unification.[7]

Now it was France's turn to bridle: a Hohenzollern enthroned in Madrid would have meant that Prussia was effectively assuming access to the

Atlantic and Mediterranean as well as confronting its southern border across the Pyrenees. This hit a raw nerve left exposed since the bloody wars with the Spanish Habsburgs in the seventeenth century: the general response in France was one of outrage, and Louis Napoléon felt that he should capitalize on it. If France gave any ground on this issue, perhaps the Prussians would also be emboldened to stake some claim to the buffer zone of Belgium.

The Prussians were, of course, only playing a provocative game: they were not seriously interested in Spain and quietly dropped the Hohenzollern claim, but they remained seriously interested in trumping the French. When the French ambassador was sent to the spa town of Bad Ems, where the king of Prussia was taking the waters, to demand further concessions (including a commitment to renounce all claim to Spain in perpetuity), King Wilhelm politely but firmly refused to consider them. In what we would now describe as a leak, a cunningly redacted telegram reporting the episode, sent "confidentially" to Bismarck, found its way into the press. The Ems telegram, as it became known, deliberately made it sound as if the ambassador had been contemptuously snubbed and France's honor disparaged.

Although Emile Ollivier favored peace and proposed a cut in the military budget, most of France was now up in arms, fueled by the popular feeling that if the Prussians were spoiling for a fight, they should have one. At sixty-two, Louis Napoléon was plodding, overweight, and debilitated by persistent urinary infections and inoperable gallstones. He must have realized that time was running out: if he wanted to secure the Empire for his beloved fifteen-year-old son, Louis, he would have to personally lead the army to *la gloire*.[8]

His military commanders declared themselves battle ready, and diplomats banked on the Austrians joining the fray in revenge for Sadowa (actually, they stayed neutral, enraged by the betrayal of Maximilian and perhaps sensing that their bread would be more generously buttered by Bismarck). The fearsomely bellicose Eugénie was gung-ho, as were the majority of the press and public, to the point at which cautious or dissenting voices in government could be ignored. War credits were voted through, and the raucously patriotic Marseillaise, long banned as leftist and incendiary, was chanted on every street corner as flags were waved and crowds cheered the departure of the troops.

When the French won a tiny and insignificant skirmish at the border town of Saarbrucken, it was reported as if it were Armageddon; Paris went mad with elation. But the news soon darkened as it emerged that the enemy had literally stolen a march by using the railways to mobilize, and major French defeats at Wissembourg on August 4, 1870, at Spicheren on August 5, and at Fröschwiller on August 6 could not be glossed over. Crazy rumors and counter-rumors created further waves of panic. The fact was that Alsace was lost and Lorraine was in dire peril. Wise heads realized that the war was lost: "Without a miracle, we are done for," wrote the playwright Ludovic Halévy in his diary. "This is the end of the Empire. One may not mind much about that, but supposing this also means the end of France?" "This country deserves to be punished and I fear it will be," wrote an even grimmer Gustave Flaubert to his correspondent George Sand. "The Prussians are right. I feel we are entering blackest darkness."[9]

What was fast becoming clear was that the army was not battle ready at all. As it advanced sluggishly through Alsace toward the northeast border, it emerged that there were crucial shortages not only of necessities such as maps, bread ovens, and horse tack but also of ammunition. The French armaments were simply not up to the scale of the job: never mind the mechanical problems that beset the *mitrailleuse;* there were not enough of them anyway. At the helm, Louis Napoléon was listless, sapless, and almost diffident as his two equally creaky field marshals Bazaine and MacMahon squabbled over tactics. Meanwhile, the Prussian machine had smoothly revved up, and Bismarck had received support from other German states. The army that resulted was highly disciplined and meticulously organized along a single chain of command, backed by a seamless chain of supply and the resources of heavy industry, including the mighty Krupp cannon that had made such an emphatic impression at the *Exposition universelle* three years previously.

On August 18 came the first catastrophe. Following a massive defeat at Gravelotte, the forces under Bazaine were driven back to the town of Metz, where they were besieged by 150,000 Prussian troops. En route to relieve Bazaine, Louis Napoléon and MacMahon suffered a similar fate— after a fiasco at Beaumont, they retreated to the town of Sedan, where the Prussians could easily encircle them. "We're stuck in a chamber pot, and they're about to shit on us," as one commander admitted. So they did. The battle that ensued on September 1 was all too predictably a disaster for the French, and by the evening Louis Napoléon, his cheeks rouged to mask his deathly pallor, gave the order to hoist the white flag of surrender. "I haven't even managed to get myself killed," he shrugged. He then sent a message to the king of Prussia: "Having failed to meet death in the midst of my troops, nothing remains for me but to yield up my sword into Your Majesty's hands."

After a brief parley with Bismarck and the granting of his wish that he should not be made to pass through the ranks of his vanquished army, Louis Napoléon became a prisoner of war in a requisitioned château, informed that he would be kept hostage until a satisfactory peace agreement was secured. He then retired to bed with his usual sangfroid and read a few pages of a historical novel by Edward Bulwer-Lytton before falling asleep.[10]

Two days later, after weeks of furious rioting in Paris and the declaration of a provisional Government of National Defense, the Second Empire simply crumbled away without abdication being necessary. Eugénie fled the Tuileries via a back door of the Louvre, taking shelter with her sympathetic American dentist until she could disguise herself—as a lunatic being transported from an asylum—and surreptitiously make her way, like Charles X and Louis-Philippe before her, across the Channel from Deauville to England.

After a period in captivity, Louis Napoléon was released by the Prussians and allowed to follow her. He and Eugénie settled in the Kentish village of Chislehurst, renting a relatively modest mansion that today has been converted into a golf clubhouse. Louis Napoléon died a broken man in 1873, and with the death of his precious son, Loulou, the prince impérial, six years later during the Zulu Wars, the direct line of the Bonaparte dynasty expired. Eugénie lived on indomitably until 1920 and the age of ninety-four—long enough to see the end of the First World War and France's recovery of territory lost to the Prussians in 1870.[11]

7

PARIS'S CIVIL WAR

THROUGHOUT THE WAR, THE WORLD looked on aghast. Opinion among Protestant nations was largely on the side of the Prussians, their sober industry being primly compared to French laxity. As George Eliot wrote sententiously,

> I am very sorry for the sufferings of the French nation. But I think these sufferings are better for the moral welfare of the people than victory would have been. . . . The war has been drawn down on them by an iniquitous government, but in a great proportion of the French people there has been nourished a wicked glorification of selfish pride, which like all other conceit is a sort of stupidity, excluding any true conception of what lies outside their own vain wishes.[1]

Britain, Austria, and Russia all refused to intervene, either diplomatically or militarily: France would have to pay the price of its own self-inflicted folly.

The tide of opinion would turn, but not yet. Throughout early September 1870, Paris was in a schizophrenic frenzy—half-terrified at the prospect of what the Prussians would do next, half-elated at the collapse of the Empire and the restoration of republicanism. Victor Hugo, author of *Les Misérables* and the French people's most revered moralist, returned to Paris after nineteen years of self-imposed exile in the Channel Islands in protest against Louis Napoléon's regime and was hailed at the Gare du Nord like a conquering hero as he hopefully proclaimed the triumph of liberty, equality, and fraternity. Some believed that a siege of Paris was inconceivable, others that it was all too likely.

But as the Prussians appeared to be advancing inexorably from the East without meeting resistance, General Trochu, doubling as president of the new republic and governor of Paris, mobilized the militia of the Garde Nationale to defend the capital. This was a body of 300,000 men conscripted from all walks of life who were given basic training in patrolling the city's impressive defenses—a thick encircling wall, 10 meters (33 feet) high, with nearly a hundred bastions and a deep ditch, as well as sixteen detached forts beyond it, forming a ring of over 40 kilometers (25 miles). But arming this body in even the most rudimentary way was taking a big risk: as left-wing red factions spread disaffection and demands throughout the working class, the loyalty of conscripts to the new government could not be guaranteed.

By September 19, the Prussians had impenetrably ringed the entire city, and the waiting game began. Mail could now leave the city only by balloon or pigeon; all exit routes were closed. Only the Americans maintained diplomatic relations with the besiegers, and their legation managed to organize a last exodus of foreign citizens through the lines. Adamantly insisting on unconditional surrender and the secession of Alsace and Lorraine, Bismarck continued to resist all the entreaties for a negotiated peace, nonchalantly puffing on a cigar as Vice President Jules Favre burst into maudlin tears and stated, "You are trying to destroy France!"

Besieged Metz fell to the Prussians, evaporating any hope that Paris might be relieved by Bazaine's army. Casualty levels were catastrophically high: by the end of October, the great majority of France's soldiers either lay hastily buried in Alsace,

Lorraine, or Champagne or moldered in prisoner-of-war camps. Morale in the capital plummeted further with the miserable failure of an attempt at a mass breakout in the South, aimed at joining up with French forces still at liberty near Orléans. After the carnival of excitement and extravagance they had enjoyed throughout the Second Empire, Parisians began to suffer from a variety of cabin fever, compounded by dread of what would happen over the winter if the situation did not change and bombardment began.

By December, as temperatures dropped below freezing point, fuel was at a premium. Food supplies ran ever lower, although one product that remained uselessly plentiful was jars of Colman's mustard. Bread was rationed despite previous official statements that the stock of flour was unlimited. Not only horses but also dogs and cats and even hapless camels and elephants in the zoo were slaughtered for meat. Garbage was piling high in the streets, and the death rate rose alarmingly as disease and illness flourished among the vulnerable poor: an outbreak of smallpox caused more than a thousand deaths.

On December 27 the Prussians started a random bombardment. Even though in the era before

One of the few surviving photographs of the Siege of Paris, during which balloons were used in attempts to send communications beyond the enemy's lines. (NADAR / HULTON ARCHIVE / GETTY IMAGES)

dynamite a bombardment was more of a noisy nuisance than a deadly menace, the explosions only emphasized the deterioration of the situation and the helplessness of the city's defenses. General Trochu, governor of Paris and ultimately answerable to the feeble and divided provisional government based in Tours, continued to maintain a stance based on the rhetoric of unremitting defiance. He claimed that he had a "plan," but fewer and fewer people believed him, especially after the ghastly failure of another bungled attempt to break out in the West of the city. Inexorably and toxically, most of those who were roundly fed up, hungry, and worried were drawn toward the firebrands of the harder left and their calls for a new strategy. Walls were posted with a proclamation:

Has the government charged with national defence fulfilled its mission? NO! . . . Through its slowness, its indecision, its inertia, those who govern us have led us to the brink of an abyss. They do not know how to administrate or fight. . . . The politics, the strategy, the administration of the government of 4 September, heirs to the Empire, are doomed. Surrender to the people! Surrender to the Commune!

The Commune was an idea that was fast gaining ground—a radically democratic breakaway government of the people of Paris for the people for Paris, full of those madly ready to rush out and storm the Prussian lines with whooping war cries: anything to break the unremitting tension of daily waiting. The amateur soldiers of the part-time Garde Nationale patrolling the city walls were worse than ineffectual, with daily reports of their drunken incompetence and dereliction of duty. The fact that most of them were also armed with rifles, bayonets, and pistols, and some had access to heavier armaments and explosives, made them potentially combustible.

Through January 1871, the tragedy built to a catastrophic climax. The Prussians trounced another French force near Le Mans, and the bombardment of Paris intensified. With his stock at its zenith, Bismarck took advantage of his occupation of the palace of Versailles to realize his greatest aim—the unity of all the German states, both Catholic and Protestant, in a new nation firmly dominated by Prussia. On January 18 the inauguration of the Second German Reich was proclaimed in an elaborate ceremony in Louis XIV's Hall of Mirrors, during which King Wilhelm of Prussia was crowned Kaiser, or emperor, with Bismarck as his "Iron Chancellor." The insult to France could hardly have been more pointed.

Stolid and pious, Trochu announced that Geneviève, the city's patron saint, had appeared to him in a vision promising last-minute salvation, but even this was not enough to save him. "I am the Jesus Christ of the situation," he lamented after his cabinet insisted he resign.[2] When disaffected members of the Garde Nationale then raided the Mazas prison and released some of their comrades, something snapped. Thousands marched on the Hôtel de Ville to demand a change of course and personnel: among the most belligerent was the fearsome feminist and anarchist Louise Michel, attired like Joan of Arc in male uniform. Shouting and confusion ensued, shots were fired randomly, and five protesters ended up being killed in the fracas. An unstoppable insurrection—perhaps another revolution—seemed imminent, fueled by famine. There was no alternative but to propose an armistice and talk peace with Bismarck—the problem being that this move was only a secret decision of the cabinet controlling Paris, not the national government based in Tours. And the people of Paris did not want surrender: as the bombardment of the city intensified, they thundered their implacable resistance *à outrance,* to the death.

Via a message covertly delivered to a Prussian outpost, a brief truce was negotiated that allowed Paris's acting president, Jules Favre, safe conduct to sneak out of Paris down the Seine in a leaky boat and thence to Bismarck's headquarters in Versailles. After the usual bluffing and posturing on both sides, the terms of an armistice were agreed. The Prussians would be paid an indemnity of 200 million francs, the outlying forts would be surrendered, and the French regular army inside the city would lay down all its arms except for officers' swords. However, Favre did secure significant concessions: no prisoners of war would be taken out of the country, and to avoid rioting or worse, the Garde Nationale would be permitted to keep its motley collection of rifles, muskets, and pistols. At midnight on January 26, in a gesture of honor, Paris was permitted to fire one final shell into the night sky before hostilities ceased and all fell silent.

The following morning a proclamation was posted. With the remainder of France's army held at bay, there was no prospect of relieving the siege, and even emergency supplies of basic foodstuffs were apparently exhausted: "In these circumstances negotiation is the absolute duty of the government." In other words, Paris had fallen and should now await its sentence.

Mysteriously and without overt restocking, food immediately reappeared on the streets in abundance and prices dropped, suggesting that a considerable amount of hoarding had been taking place. Within a couple of weeks, railway lines had reopened, and the gas supply was restored. Foreign journalists entered the city and reported that there had been "a great deal of exaggeration about the actual horrors of the siege," but how much did they see?[3] The bourgeois, Haussmannized West may have been wearily resigned and hoping for a return to normality, but the proletarian East, swollen with hordes of migrant workers who were attracted to the city by Haussmann's projects and were then left high and dry and fatally unemployed, was less sanguine.[4]

Politically, the priority was to establish a government legally empowered to negotiate a lasting peace treaty, but given the intense factionalism inside and outside Paris, that would be no easy task. An election in early February resulted in a conservative administration led by the cold, clever, and calculating Thiers, who had sat out the siege in

Tours and had little idea of what was going on in the capital—crucially, he underestimated the fighting spirit of leftist factions opposed to any sellout to the Prussians and rightly suspicious that some sort of humiliation (an occupation, financial penalties) might be on the table as a bargaining chip in peace negotiations. As a precaution and to make its intentions plain, an alliance of battalions within the Garde Nationale decided to corral hundreds of cannon bought by public subscription for the city's defense on "safe" sites in Montmartre and Belleville. On the same day a mob lynched a police spy on the Place de la Bastille, dragging him down to the Seine, where he was strangled and drowned.

Then came the news of the proposed peace terms: France was to yield Alsace-Lorraine to the German Reich and pay a gigantic indemnity of 5,000 million francs (in 5-franc pieces, it was calculated, this would have produced a column 2,500 kilometers or 1,550 miles high). However, what outraged Paris the most was a clause permitting 30,000 Prussian troops limited but symbolic entry to the center of the capital until the new parliamentary assembly ratified the terms of the treaty.

As if holding their collective breath, everyone but the drunks and the urchins behaved impeccably through the dreadful forty-eight hours of March 1 and 2, 1871. The streets were empty, the Arc de Triomphe was blocked off, no newspapers were published, no omnibuses ran, shops closed their shutters, and black veils were cast over statues of French heroes. On the Bois de Boulogne, the Kaiser solemnly reviewed troops, who then marched down the Champs Elysées to the Place de la Concorde. Bismarck had the nerve to ask a Frenchman for a light and then puffed glacially on his habitual cigar. The troops were at leisure to enjoy the sights and wander; on the following day, they even began to strike up friendly conversations with a few curious natives who had ventured out. On March 3 the treaty was ratified, and the Prussians marched out with the same discipline that they had shown two days earlier. Calm had been maintained, but Paris felt that its nose had been rubbed in the ordure of its defeat.

Moving into Versailles after Bismarck's departure and thinking to avoid any more trouble, Thiers's right-wing government misread the mood by turning sharply nasty and intensifying censorship and surveillance. Among a series of draconian economic measures designed to raise levies sufficient to pay off the first tranche of that massive

A barricade thrown up during the Commune. Note the presence of women and children. (Keystone-France / Gamma-Keystone via Getty Images).

indemnity, the daily allowance doled out to the Garde Nationale was stopped, in effect rendering many of its members completely destitute. But the spark that ignited the catastrophe was an order that the Garde's beloved cannon should be requisitioned by the regular army. The military operation aimed at reclamation that took place on March 18 was a fiasco: Thiers's soldiers mutinied as the Garde rallied to preserve what it justifiably considered to be the property of the people of Paris, and as the red flag was defiantly hoisted, two generals were taken hostage and summarily shot.[5]

Terrified of inflaming the situation, Thiers withdrew all his troops, in effect abandoning Paris to anarchy, and for a couple of days mobs rioted and plundered as barricades were erected and public buildings were occupied and ransacked. Nobody knew what was going on or what to do next: some parts of the city seemed completely tranquil, but others were in a constant ferment of violence and lawlessness. Only a precarious and penniless committee of the Garde Nationale attempted to keep order through its ability to bring some of the factions into fragile unity. From a base in which representation was proportionately weighted toward the working-class areas, an autonomous city government, popularly referred to as the Commune, was elected and formally declared on March 28.

This sudden power grab by the Parisian underclass, seizing back what Louis Napoléon and Haussmann's cleansing and the Prussians had expropriated, was not something even the most romantic revolutionary could seriously have expected a year previously, and not surprisingly a sense of chronic insecurity would underlie everything the Commune would do, dream, or decree over the coming weeks. How long could this last? was the unspoken, unthinkable, yet unavoidable question for those standing on the edge of a precipice with nowhere else to move.

Sixty-four men took office on March 28, 1871, all of them left-wing idealists; twenty-one further moderates, elected at the same time, had immediately resigned because they felt unable to stomach coalition or collaboration. Of those remaining, half were skilled artisans and over half under the age of thirty-three. Only a quarter of them were born in Paris; eighteen were middle class, a few were intellectuals, and a few were eccentric bordering on the lunatic. The name, let alone the philosophy, of Karl Marx was virtually unknown to them; instead, they espoused a wide variety of socialist doctrines, some vaporously mystical, some aggressively atheistic, but almost all staunchly opposed to the Catholic establishment (one wag anticipated the Dada movement by half a century when he stuck a pipe into the mouth of a statue of the Virgin Mary). As a band, they were portrayed by their enemies and the press as corrupt opportunists and murderous villains, but the evidence is that the worst one could say of the great majority of them is that their sincerity was fatally naive. Venal they certainly were not—their bookkeeping accounted for every last *sou*.

They had no leader: theirs would be a rule of extreme democracy, which of course meant a dearth of clear decision making and a glut of dead-end meetings and debates, fissures, and fractures. With the odds stacked impossibly high against them, nobody had any clear idea of how to consolidate their overall position, while everybody had his own ideas about which issues should take priority. Starry-eyed high-mindedness was initially the keynote: "*Debout, les damnés de la terre . . . C'est l'eruption de la fin, Le monde va changer de base*" went the apocalyptic new anthem ("Rise up, ye cursed of the Earth . . . it's the final explosion, the world is changing from its foundations"), and for a moment the world seemed to be turning upside down as traditional authority was knocked off its throne and the humble and meek were exalted. Moratoriums on debt and rent were declared, the poor were succored, workers' cooperatives were encouraged, and the rights of women were extended, but the lack of any rigorous administrative substructure meant that few of these measures were ever properly tested or implemented. And, paradoxically, as a state of emergency prevailed, fundamental constitutional liberties were simultaneously suspended: compulsory identity cards were introduced, and one law stated vaguely that "any person suspected of complicity with the government of Versailles will be immediately charged and incarcerated"—in other words, anybody could be arrested for just about anything. Paranoia about spies and fifth-column conspiracies was as rampant as the spread of what we now call fake news. Yet the screws had to be turned tight because Versailles was bombarding the center of the city from hills on the outskirts, and it was an open secret that a major assault was being prepared.

Thiers was not in a hurry: by now he had realized that the cancer of Paris's disaffection required careful surgical attention and that his administration, scarcely less young and fragile than that of the Commune, was not really qualified to deal with it. He could not afford to rush into another failure, so over the coming weeks he would focus on refining his strategy, correcting shortages in equipment, and drilling loyalty and morale back into his battered army.

Had he dared to wait longer, the Commune might well have fragmented to the point of imploding. By mid-April, its impetus had already begun to falter, and ordinary folk were increasingly disgruntled as the promised bright day was evidently not dawning. With the economy in a slump, there was not enough for people to do, and hanging around talking about the latest rumor sapped morale. By-elections in the constituencies vacated by the withdrawn moderates drew dismally low turnouts, and although produce could enter the city easily enough, food prices were skyrocketing. Resignations followed slanderous accusations of treason and the connivance of stool pigeons. The arguments were incessant, with only the freemasons making a plucky but inconsequential attempt to conciliate the Versaillais. Outside Paris, the French prayed for a negotiated settlement; surely there were rights and wrongs on both sides, and enough blood had already been spilled without the peculiar horror of a massacre of compatriots.

The legislation proposed in the Commune's endlessly proliferating committees and political clubs became increasingly daft—for example, the compulsory teaching of a universal language, a purge of prostitution, and the abolition of all titles and liveries. However, silliest of all was the destruction on May 16 of the triumphal column in the Place Vendôme that commemorated Napoléon's campaigns and *la gloire* of modern France—a symbolic gesture of singular futility that enraged old soldiers and made the Communards look like vandals. Far more ominous, stoking paranoia about fifth columnists, was the following day's inexplicable explosion of an armory near the Champ de Mars, thunderously destroying millions of cartridges, exploding silos of gunpowder, and casting a vast pall of smoke over the city.

On May 22 the Commune's death knell was sounded when 130,000 orderly Versaillais troops breached the walls of Paris and occupied the west side of the city within twenty-four hours, slowly preparing an assault on the revolutionary strongholds of Montmartre and Belleville in the Northeast. At first there was little resistance: the Commune had no firm military leadership or plans with which to counter this invasion, and such barricades as were erected in the back streets were thrown up haphazardly. The posters rallying the proletariat to the cause's last ditch were hysterical and desperate: "Make way for the people, for fighters, for bare arms! The people know nothing of intricate manoeuvres, but when they have a gun in hand, paving stones underneath them, they have no fear at all of all the strategists of the monarchical school. To arms, citizens!"

Some hoped that the Versailles army would desert en masse to their true brothers and sisters, but its soldiers were well primed, well fed, and unmoved by the call to solidarity with the losing side. Inexorably, they advanced along Haussmann's broad boulevards as Thiers declared in hollow rhetoric to his parliamentary assembly that any purge would be enacted "in the name of the law and by the law." The reality was simple: just shoot to kill.

Then the fires began. Most of the major monuments on the Right Bank—the Palais-Royal, the Tuileries, the ministries, the Prefecture of Police, the department stores, the Gobelins tapestry manufactory—were engulfed in a spiraling inferno. Also gutted was the Hôtel de Ville, a major loss to historians being its files of paperwork relating to Haussmann's projects. "We could not but recall some passages in the 18th chapter of the Book of Revelation," wrote an American chaplain, William Gibson, witness to the awesome spectacle. The newspapers claimed that marauding bands of wild, coarse, degenerate females carrying matches and jerricans of paraffin were responsible, but not one of these mythical creatures—identified in the press as *pétroleuses*—was ever apprehended. Yet whether by accident or design, the conflagration would rage for days.

As all semblance of moral boundaries vanished, any pretence of official justice administered through tribunals proved hollow: a person's life or death became a matter of someone else's momentary whim. Following a slaughter of prisoners by the Versaillais, the Commune shot in reprisal six hostage clergymen, including the archbishop of Paris, who instantly became a globally mourned martyr. Pandemonium took over. Any faint pretext of rational revenge then gave way to blind, mad murder, with no mercy shown on either side toward those who laid down their arms and surrendered. The Commune shot a further fifty-one hostages, peppering one body with sixty-nine bullets; the Versaillais dragged three hundred people out of sanctuary in the church of the Madeleine and killed them all. A particularly savage end was that meted out to Tony Moilin, a selfless doctor and dedicated socialist who wrote a utopian book imagining Paris as it might be in the year 2000 (a brave new world complete with social housing and aerial railways). As mayor of his arrondissement, he was arraigned before a summary court-martial and condemned to death not for any culpable action but merely for his leftist reputation. The judge "mercifully" allowed him a respite of twelve hours to marry his heavily pregnant partner, Lucie, before he was executed in the Jardin de Luxembourg.

Over the next few nightmare days, 147 men were felled by the rat-a-tat-tat volley of the *mitrailleuse* against a wall in the cemetery of Père Lachaise, still marked today as the Mur des Fédérés. Elsewhere, groups of twenty were lined up and summarily wiped out in barracks, railway stations, schoolyards, and even public squares. A hospital set up at Saint-Sulpice was blasted. A thousand corpses were said to be piled up at the Trocadéro, while three hundred more were dumped into the pretty artificial lake at the heart of Haussmann's park at the Buttes-Chaumont—dragged out days later, bloated and putrid, they were flung on a stinking funeral pyre that burned and festered for weeks. Columns of refugees attempted to flee the chaos by every route out of the city, but all passages to safety were blocked, leaving helpless innocents, including thousands of parentless children, all assuming that they were destined for the firing squad, forced on marches into vast concentration compounds on the city's outskirts.

The figures behind what amounted to a week of massacre more brutal than anything in French history—known to posterity as *la semaine sanglante* (the bloody week)—remain much disputed, but Versailles would admit to causing 17,000 "fatalities," and even the more conservative estimates reckon on at least 3,000 more. Rough and repressive justice followed. Following nearly 380,000 letters from ordinary citizens denouncing other ordinary citizens, some 40,000 people associated with the Commune would be held in hulks and perfunctorily tried over the next four years, resulting in 13,000 guilty verdicts. Of these, 23 were shot or guillotined, 251 were sentenced to forced labor for life, and about 5,000 were transported to the tropical horrors of New Caledonia. The more civilized world looked on with appalled contempt at such kangaroo-court proceedings, and Gladstone flatly refused to extradite those Communards who had managed to escape across the Channel to England.[6]

But Paris deserved its comeuppance, people commonly said: a city of decadence and extravagance that had given in to self-indulgence, poisoned by the bohemian evils of venereal disease, drunkenness, and democracy. The Second Empire had allowed morality to be abandoned, and the Commune

was the outcome. The country as a whole had much
to learn from the Prussian example, argued the distinguished theologian Ernest Renan in *La Réforme
intellectuelle et morale de la France*. Racists pointed
to the implications of the declining birth rate and
called for a purification of miscegenated French
stock; Catholics talked of Sodom and Gomorrah.
In 1873 the first pilgrimage to Lourdes took place;
there was much talk of Joan of Arc and the spirit
of the nation. From his home near Rouen, Gustave Flaubert lamented cynically that "Paris wasn't
burned to the last house, leaving only a black void.
France has fallen so low, is so dishonoured, so de-
based, that I wish she might disappear completely."
After visiting the city, he added that "the odour of
the corpses disgusted me less than the miasmas of
egotism exhaled from every mouth. The sight of the
ruins is as nothing compared to the immense Parisian stupidity."[7]

Yet Paris recovered, at least superficially, with
astonishing alacrity. Dismantling of the barricades,
cobbling the ripped-up streets, and reconstructing
the burned-out buildings of state began almost
immediately—only the palace of the Tuileries was
left to rot, standing like Shelley's statue of Ozyman-
dias as a warning to all who passed of the vanity of

imperial power (not until 1889 would its walls be razed and the site transformed into the public park that exists today). The middle-class residential area west of the city, spared the arson and relatively unscathed by the fighting, resumed the appearance of normality within weeks, as the cafés and restaurants of the Champs Elysées bustled with rubbernecking tourists flocking to stare at the "new Pompeii" while clutching a guidebook, *A travers les ruines de Paris,* that had been opportunistically rushed to press to meet demand. Few of them can have ventured to the bleaker prospects of Montmartre or Belleville, where a surly vacant silence prevailed among the vanquished survivors and martial law enforced a curfew amid police crackdowns on the ordinary vices of prostitution and drunken disorderliness that kept many poor people functioning. The wounds here would take decades to heal and were still vividly cited and honored almost a century later when the students took to the streets during the events of 1968.

In 1875 the constitution of the Third Republic was confirmed, and a new phase of French history began under a political dispensation that would endure until 1940, when the Germans returned to occupy Paris as Nazis. With the indemnity to Prussia paid off much more speedily and less painfully than anyone expected, trade and employment picked up. *Paris s'amuse*. Shorn of its imperial trimmings, Garnier's splendiferous Opéra (which had served as a hospital and a store during the hostilities) opened with flourish and fanfare, as we saw at the beginning of this book. Renoir painted *Les grands boulevards*, one of that year's crop of Impressionist paintings, showing a sunny urban scene devoid of political tensions or signs of conflict. By 1878, the year of a glorious exhibition on the Champ de Mars that displayed prototypes of the electric refrigerator, telephone, and phonograph and drew 13 million visitors from all corners of the civilized world, Henry James could write that "Paris is today in outward aspect as radiant [and] as prosperous . . . as if her sky had never known a cloud."[8]

The widowed Eugénie and the prince impérial (wearing the uniform of a cadet of the Royal Military Academy in Woolwich) in the garden of Camden Place, Chislehurst, their home in suburban Kent during their English exile. (CHRISTOPHEL FINE ART / UIG VIA GETTY IMAGES)